r 1,99

CW00952224

Wipe the slate clean

by Marc Isenschmid

www.doorsofconsciousness.com

Thanks to my wife and children to be in my life.

About the Author

Born in 1974, Marc Isenschmid is a holistic practitioner and teacher based in Switzerland.

Eclectic and self-taught, he showed, from an early age, an interest in many different fields. Passionate about writing, he studied journalism at the University of Fribourg (Switzerland) before devoting himself to designing websites and developing his skills in design and computer science.

At 25, after experiencing an amazing cure following a treatment using a natural therapy, he decided to change his career to become a holistic practitioner himself.

He started to study different natural medicine techniques and after several years of practice, he designed his own healing and personal development method called "Doors of Consciousness".

He has since been teaching this method through various training courses in addition to working as a holistic practitioner.

Marc is married with three children.

TABLE OF CONTENTS

PREAMBLE

Beliefs are sentences in your head.
For example :
« I am the best » or
« I am a failure » or
« Love hurts ».

Every adult has hundred of thousands of beliefs.
They are codes, 0 and 1, inside your body, your cells, your mind, your soul. Not just opinion, programs.

They can create a reality. Like in the matrix. Some people live an easy life, some live a very difficult one. Beliefs can explain such differences.

They have the power to alter your mind, your willpower, your health, your relationships, your success, your reflexes.

If you want to change something in your life, it's the place to start.
If you want to heal, it's the place to start.
If you want to be better, well, you know the music.

Other methods will propose to replace them with better beliefs. I will suggest something different. We have so many beliefs, 99% of them is junk, toxic sentences that alter your life. Just delete them!

How? This is the purpose of this book.

How to erase? How to do that in a safe way? How to be quick and efficient? How to obtain results?

Take the red pill.

WHAT IS THE DIFFERENCE BETWEEN A FACT AND A BELIEF?

Facts are rare. Scientific truths, we can call facts, are difficult to find. Scientists use axioms, facts that can be observed in a systematic way but cannot be mathematically proven. For example, the shortest path between two points is a straight line. This axiom is a fact because it can be verified in every experience you have.

You can find other facts, mostly scientific truths, which have been demonstrated by a large number (tens of thousands) of iterations (repetitions):

Fact: "The Earth revolves around the Sun".
Fact: "Gravity exists".

A fact can be challenged when our measuring instruments improve and when our scientific understanding of the world is increasing. Before *Galileo* and *Copernic*, *"the sun revolved around the earth"*. It was a fact you could see every day. This proves that even a fact is not as certain as it seems. However, we can at least use a fact to build something and find some reassurance from it.

Any fact, which is not identical to each observation (iteration), regardless of the number of observations, is what I call a **recurrence.** An event repeating itself 98 times out of a 100 is a statistical truth, a recurrence, however this is not a fact.

Deducing a general truth from a recurrence is what I call a belief.

A belief is the lost cousin of the scientific fact. It has its flavor and appearance, but it certainly is not a fact. To adopt a belief, we only need *hearsay,* personal experiences, distorted deductions, statistics and second hand opinions such as "I have read in a medical journal..." or "I've seen on TV...". We only base ourselves on a few repetitions to prove our beliefs.

A belief is an idea, a concept, an opinion, something we wish to defend. There are probably as many beliefs as there are "objects" in our lives. And by "object" I mean: an idea, an emotion, a person, a tree, a table...

A belief is also a peremptory statement.

Some beliefs follow facts and cling to them like a plastic film. For example, we can "believe" that the earth revolves around the sun or we can "believe" in gravity. That does not mean that the phenomenon exists. When we stop believing in them, facts remain. Therefore it is easy to get confused and mix facts with beliefs.

Examples of beliefs:
The statement "A mother always loves her child" is a belief. Why? Because it is a recurrence, not a systematic fact. There are exceptions to this statement, as the police and social services know.
To say: "I am not good at anything" is a belief. You can

believe it but you cannot prove it scientifically.

"Life is hard" is a belief based on many difficult experiences inherited from our ancestors coupled with our own recurrences, however it is not a scientific fact.

"This medicine always works" is also a belief. A remedy's effectiveness is expressed in percentage. When it reaches a certain level of effectiveness with minimal side effects, it may be marketed. It is only a recurrence.

"I am convinced that the earth revolves around the sun" is a belief. The words we use to express a fact reveals a belief. Everything is in the wording.

"Natural birth is better than a Caesarean section" is a belief. There may be statistical studies proving this, but where there is a statistical proof there is a recurrence, therefore there could be exceptions. The simple fact that some people try to defend this claim proves that a belief exists.

If you think about this, you will probably realize that there are two types of beliefs, i.e., those that are established by a fact and those that are not.

A belief proved by a fact is acceptable but unnecessary in the sense that facts exist by themselves. Therefore, those beliefs have no reason to exist.

A belief that is not proven by a fact is false, or even detrimental as it restrains your thoughts. Those beliefs should not exist.

My aim is to help you erase your beliefs.

How does that sound?

WHAT ARE BELIEFS?

NATURE OF BELIEFS

Above all, we must make one thing clear: <u>beliefs are sentences</u>.

Beliefs are ideas, concepts that we have in our unconscious mind. You can hear them in your thoughts and in your words, <u>when the unconscious is getting conscious</u>.

A belief is always a statement.

For example:
"I am not good at Maths"
"Nobody loves me"
"Life is unfair"

On the contrary, expressing a condition or an emotion is not a belief but sometimes the difference is subtle. When we say: "I feel tired", we recognize our state of mind, when we say "I feel sad", we express an emotion but when we say, "I feel that I will never get out of this situation", we express a belief.

Not everything you say is a belief, however all statements using "I am like that, I believe this, I am sure of it, it is my conviction that, it is like that, I am

convinced that, it is not possible, I do not believe it, I feel that ..." are beliefs.

If you listen to your words, you can easily find your beliefs. And it is even easier to find those when you listen to someone else. However, you will not be able to see how widespread these beliefs are in our lives. This is the first issue because if you cannot see them, you cannot accept them for what they really are.

Let's talk about some characteristics of beliefs:

1. The essence of a belief is that we think it is true

This axiom is fundamental. A belief is not confined to be a silly superstition. In most cases, a belief is based on a personal experience, a recurrence or a scientific fact.

Our need to generalize and to be right is driving us to create or adopt a belief.

Society is full of beliefs that may seem true or "very reasonable" to us:

For example:
Men are stronger than women.
Men are rational and women intuitive.
Human beings are superior to animals.
Suffering is here to help us evolve.
Money cannot buy happiness.
Being spontaneous is dangerous.
Intelligent people are more likely to succeed in life than others.
Life is hard, you must keep fighting.

We must be punished to better understand our mistakes or faults.

If people had no beliefs, there would be no morality.

If people no longer believed in good or evil, anarchy would spread.

Exercise

Do you agree with any of these beliefs? If so, why do you agree? What do you use to prove that these beliefs are true? Your own experience, the experience of somebody else, the opinion of others? Try to grade how true these claims are on a scale of 0 to 10, 0 = FALSE, 10 = totally TRUE. Among these beliefs, which one was true before but not now? What made you change your mind? Note that it is possible to score how true these statements are (from 1 to 10).

2. We want to believe that we must believe

Generally speaking, we live in a society where beliefs are seen as necessary.

For example:

You must believe in yourself.

Believing is succeeding.

Believing is putting all odds on your side.

To succeed you must believe.

To pass this test, you must believe.

To get this job you must believe.

Those who fail are those who do not believe enough in them to succeed.

You must believe in something.

Believing is making me secure.

My beliefs are part of my identity.

Beliefs help me understand the difference between good and bad.

Believing makes things work.

Think positive, you must believe in a positive outcome.

You can hear so many of these sentences and more in the mouth of your neighbors, your friends, your family or yourself. These statements are beliefs. But are they true? How relevant are they?

I guess you probably experienced a failure where you were sure of your success or, on the contrary, you may have achieved something in your life without really believing in it. So, if there are exceptions, why do you believe in this kind of things?

Exercise

- Why do you believe that we must believe?

- Why do you believe that success depends on the strength of your belief?

- Do you believe in positive thinking and if so, why?

- Are you able to justify it with a scientifically proven fact?

"Think positive or you will not get what you want in life" is a belief. Nothing can prove it scientifically, but this belief has spread like a virus around the world. I see two negative aspects in it.

On the one hand, this belief drives us to constantly monitor our thoughts to ensure these are always perfect. It is difficult then to find peace of mind.

It also pushes us to repress our emotions and negative thoughts somewhere. But where do we repress all of these? Are they really gone? Where do we store this negativity?

On the other hand, when we fail, it is assumed from the outset that we were not positive enough, while there are probably other answers to this failure.

Exercise
Why did I fail this? Try for once to think about your failures without worrying about this belief and really try to find a coherent and logical reason for your past or recent failures.

Clearly there are exceptions to this rule about positive thinking: some people succeed without believing, some people have confidence in themselves without "believing" in them. We can obtain a driver's license without believing and being negative about it from the start. We can obtain a good grade at school with no preparation, no positive thinking and then be surprised about the positive outcome. We can succeed in court while scared to death. A girl or a boy can answer "yes" when asked on a date even if the person asking them out is lacking confidence and does not necessarily believe they will agree to date them...

Being positive is not dangerous, but the belief that you have to think positive is dangerous as it makes you ignore what is real.

3. A belief is not a fact but it can be superimposed on a fact

Imagine a belief as a plastic film. You can laminate a fact with a belief. This does not make it truer but it reassures you. It is an unconscious process.

If you pull out the plastic film, the fact continues to exist.

You do not need this kind of belief especially if you are a scientist. Because, as you will see later, believing in something makes us ignore interesting information.

4. A belief is similar to a virus

A belief is a very small unit, a brick to build our way of thinking and acting. A belief system is a combined total functioning with one identity. Every human being is a belief system in itself, within which there are several other belief systems, all forming a block around the one topic. A belief is as small and dangerous as a virus.

It exists within us but if we communicate with others, it can spread and replicate itself. A belief is contagious.

We often say that fear is contagious. It spreads through the crowd sometimes causing stampedes when people are walking all over each other trying to escape. A belief can spread the same way.

5. A belief is not a thought but generates one

A belief is what sets the involuntary mind in motion. It is at the centre of it but it is not a thought itself. We think of it and perceive it as our thought but it's not a thought. This is important to remember. Your mind is an aspect of you that helps you think, feel, conceptualize and perceive yourself. Your mind is what allows you to "hear" your beliefs but your **beliefs are not necessarily in your mind**.

Beliefs exist at a deeper level than thoughts. Beliefs are to thoughts what genes are to the body. Precursors, originators. A programming.

For example:

A belief such as "I must be respected" creates a specific state of mind. Missing from the conscious mind under normal circumstances, this belief is empowered when you think about something or live something related to it. Once this belief is activated, you will think and imagine things like: "this is not normal, I am not respected, and I should be respected in this situation. What should I do? Impose myself? Ignore that person? Hit that person? Show him/her disrespect? Etc."

The belief "I should get angry when someone doesn't do what I want" creates an intolerant, demanding and hostile state of mind.

6. A belief generates emotions

Similarly, beliefs generate involuntary emotions.

The previous example "I must be respected" initiates emotions if or when you are not respected; emotions such as anger, frustration, sadness, regret, rage or hatred.

Often, we are not aware of this process because it happens very rapidly. It is almost imperceptible, yet if you pay attention to your emotions, you will probably identify which belief produced them.

Often these mental and emotional processes are started by several beliefs, which complicates things a little.

Use a recent event that created a deep emotional state in you and then find the beliefs that are at the source of your thoughts and emotions. Try to express these emotions aloud to yourself, using the sentences that are coming to your mind but without getting into the emotional state whilst doing it. Repeat phrases that have mentally agitated you aloud until one or more beliefs are revealed. Look for the affirmations. Take the time to do so because it is an important step to understand what I mean.

7. A belief leads to action

Most of the time, we act after thinking and feeling things. Action is rarely spontaneous. There is always something initiating it.

If you are not respected, the belief "I must be respected" will create some thoughts and emotions in you related to that. It is likely that this will also bring a need for action that you can choose to listen to or to repress. If you act, the belief is the cause of your action. If you do not act, the belief is the cause of your frustration.

8. Beliefs form complex systems

We are complex beings who create complex things. This is the same with our beliefs. These are deposited in us as silt and they eventually create a strong, rigid structure that is commonly called the belief system.

Beliefs are supporting themselves, it is very difficult to question your beliefs because each one is supported or verified by a complex set of recurrences (memories) and beliefs.

For example:

"Men are stronger than women" supports "it is men who must go to war" AND "violence is the only solution" supports "there must be war" AND "one who goes to war deserves more than one who does not" leads to "men deserve more than women" and other similar beliefs as "men should rule over women".

9. Beliefs affect our lives more than we think

If a belief is truly capable of creating thoughts and emotions, and also leads to action, then we can say that it is indirectly creative.

After having erased my beliefs, I have seen that some events no longer prevailed. It was not only tied to a mental change or a change in the way I acted or behaved, my life itself was different.

I have been able to live that experience many a times. My patients and students have been able to testify of it as well.

At this stage I realized that our beliefs were not only mental objects but also real viruses, fragments of our creation.

10. We cannot rely on beliefs to create well

We might be tempted to use beliefs to improve our life. To bring change in life, some therapy systems use "positive" beliefs. I tried to use these systems and as many others, I was rather disappointed with the results.

Beliefs do not create well, because they are unreliable, sometimes creative, sometimes not, like unnecessary deadweight. On top of that, adding beliefs to your own belief system might be conflicting and could disrupt your state of mind and emotions.

Try to believe that you will win the lottery to see if it works. Put some beliefs to the test in your life to see if they are reliable. Draw your own conclusions. Remember that a single positive result is not a proof. Sometimes elements outside of beliefs can impact on you.

ORIGINS OF BELIEFS

Our beliefs were not built in a day, our ancestors built this system day after day, experience after experience. Their need was to understand the world, to reassure themselves and find recurrences.

Let's start at the time of the supposed origin of man. The primitive man is trying to look at the world and understand how it works. He is looking for truths and relationships between cause and effect. He creates beliefs in order to have a stronger influence on his environment and because he is afraid (fear of the future, deprivation, death, loss, separation, darkness, predators...). He assumes that beliefs will help him better control the environment.

From one experience to another, man better understands his body, nature and life through repetitive patterns (recurrences). Of these schemes, he deduces beliefs that he tries to apply to practical cases. He wants to know how and why. He is no longer satisfied to live a day-to-day existence, like animals do.

Man loves his children. They come from his blood, so he tries to pass the knowledge he acquired, his experiences and his beliefs onto them.

As families expanded, they became tribes. These tribes have asserted their power and authority through their beliefs. These same beliefs became their cultural identity and as they sought to spread their identity and lifestyle, they propagated them.

These tribes settled in and bound themselves to a place and a region. As they prospered, they became ethnic groups and nations and their beliefs started to belong to their region. The first beliefs, based on survival, strength and deprivation, provided the basis of their societies.

For example:
There is not enough food for everyone.
We must have more land to be free from hunger and be safe.
We belong to the region where we came from.
The land where we are is ours.
Land can be owned.
Security means owning my land.
Power depends on the amount of land we control.
We must defend our territory.
War is the best solution.
There is not enough space in this region for both our people.
As war is necessary to possess land, the ability to go to war determines the value of a man and his ability to rule.
Being strong is necessary to go to war, therefore men must prevail not women.
As women bear children, they should have children.
Function determines fate, as shown with women childbearing.
Women should be under the rule of men.

Every month, women have their periods therefore women are sensitive to the lunar cycle.

If men are the complementary opposite of women, as proved by the complementarity of sexual organs, men are linked to the sun.

My experience is the only way to understand the world.

I lived it therefore I am right.

Old people are always right because they have lived long.

He, who knows more than us, must be our leader.

Old people are wise.

Young people are spontaneous and thoughtless.

To be spontaneous is not good.

Family is the most important thing in life.

I must be faithful to my family, my tribe and my ethnic group.

I have to respect my parents and my ancestors.

As food is in short supply, we must always finish our plates.

Food should not be wasted.

I must teach the person I love all my beliefs to help him/her live better.

Passing on knowledge (and beliefs) is important.

The only way to progress and understand things is through experience.

My past experiences help me understand what happens to me.

There is nothing more valuable than experience.

Although some of these beliefs were created more than 3'000 years ago, you can see that some of them are still valid today.

These men founded the kingdoms and empires we know: Egypt, Mesopotamia, China, India, Celts, etc.

Our own religious foundations were created around these same eras. These were inevitably influenced by social beliefs of that time. The position of women within the society is one good example. These initial beliefs were integrated and thereafter modified. Over time, religions have become more sophisticated, they created new beliefs to justify their foundation and answer questions from their believers, or to fill philosophical or logical gaps in their system.

All our societies are only building on something that was there before. The Romans (who had slaves) have directly inspired the current European legal system; the Western medical system takes from the Ancient Greeks and the Western philosophical system from both the Ancient Greeks and the Romans.

Similarly, religious systems from the West are directly inspired by religions from the Middle East: the Manichaeans (Mani, who has lived in the area of present-day Iraq and invented the "Manichaean" notion of good as opposed to evil), Judaism and Christianity.

To make it short, man recycles old beliefs to make some new ones. He will do so, for as long as he defends and values this system. Up to now, we have only known this way of doing. But why not do it differently?

EXPERIENCES AND MEMORIES

We are totally conditioned by our experiences. Indeed, the only way to understand the world seems to be through what we live. Reading, going to the cinema and the virtual reality allow us to overcome this limitation, but in general, we only believe in what we see and in what we experience.

But how do we know that our experience is TRUE: true anytime and anywhere, and which can be GENERALIZED?

Nothing.

And yet we defend our experiences.

> We are sure that cutlery must be stored head up in the dishwasher, because they get washed better that way. We believe that we must eat three meals a day to be in good health. It is proven. Our experiences, recurrences and habits make us believe that we must educate our children like this or like that because that is what we have received from our parents and "we are not so bad after all!". We are sure that accumulating wealth is the best way to feel safe because that is how our ancestors have always done it...

When we experience something, we store the event and a belief about this event. This is a reflex phenomenon.

If we live this experience repeatedly (recurring) and if we see that the causes of this experience are repeatedly the same, we will conclude that there is a relationship between cause and effect. Therefore, we create a belief or we strengthen an existing one.

Repetition gives a lot of value to a belief. It is usually enough to live two or three times the same experience to be certain that this experience is true in all cases. Which is obviously a logical mistake to make.

At best, we have deduced a relative truth, depending on other parameters (emotional state, state of mind, stress, temperature, living conditions, season, location, people with us at the time...). Therefore it is not possible to say that our experience is perfectly objective or that such a cause necessarily produces such an effect.

For example:

You know that the trip from your home to the nearest train station takes 10 minutes. You have experienced this again and again. Therefore, it is true to you. But you do not have the same perception of time as other people. Your walking or running speed is different from other people. Moreover, there are several paths to get to the station. Thus, the belief that this journey takes 10 minutes is not true in absolute terms; it is just true in some cases. From one day to another it can take you more or less time to make that journey.

You are queuing in a store. You chose the left line, which initially was shorter than the right one. But now the right line seems to move faster and the person who came up with his/her trolley will soon arrive at the till. What are you doing? Do you move to the other queue? If not, why don't you do it? Do you believe you will regret changing lines or that the queue you just left will suddenly go faster than the other one? Have you ever experienced this?

You had a car accident. This powerful event will greatly influence you. No need for a second experiment to create beliefs, this experience is so strong that it will condition you to react differently, to drive differently because you have created new beliefs.

You had a miscarriage. It is a traumatic and painful event. Because of this first miscarriage, you will see your second pregnancy differently. You will be more careful, you will be more paranoid, you will cling all the more to reassuring methods that should prevent another problem. You will be much more receptive to the beliefs of others which could help you do the best you can.

That's how we build knowledge from our experiences. That's how we create beliefs. So, will these beliefs make us think and live differently, better or be more inspired? Maybe not, but we will have more fears and we will act less spontaneously. We will use these experiences to justify our beliefs and our new attitudes.

This is why you will always use your experience to defend your beliefs. This is your way of rationalizing things, of answering when an "enemy" attempts to question one of your beliefs. However, in hindsight, you might find that you cannot generalize your experience and that just one is not representative of a scientific fact. Your experience is only one recurrence, and it should not validate your beliefs even if it is very tempting.

TRANSMISSION OF BELIEFS

Beliefs are transmitted like viruses are, from one person to another, from parents to children, from friends to friends, from media to their audiences, from a teacher to a student ... This mechanism explains the fact that you can carry beliefs fundamentally opposed to your way of thinking.

"Opposed to my way of thinking?!" you would ask me.

Yes, indeed that's possible. For example, we can believe that death is only a transition to a better world, not the definitive end of life. We could be afraid of it and avoiding it at all costs at the same time. These are inherited beliefs keeping the fear of death mixed with religious or New Age beliefs, which bring peaceful state of mind.

Expressed differently, we could simply say that our unconscious mind can have beliefs contradicting our conscious mind.

How do we pass these beliefs on?

1. By discussing or reading things

What we say and how we say it, is how we pass a belief as a

concept onto others. What you hear or what you read can give you beliefs, even if the person who told you these things or sent them to you is not aware of this mechanism and does not want to give you any belief.

2. Through education and imitation

Children absorb a lot of beliefs. Parents are their knowledge holders, they are tall, strong and can do a lot of things. Children admire their parents and all adults in general. They try to understand the world, so they turn to them to learn. "Why? Why? Why?". Often parents do not know why. But they do provide an answer, or they cheat a little and give half of the answer. Or they even completely avoid answering. However, children accept those answers, they take them as true, because they believe that adults hold the truth.

Children may initially absorb "strange" or "fun" beliefs such as Santa Claus, storks bringing babies, etc.

Secondly, school and friends will make them change their beliefs.

But at school, children will not only learn the truth, they will also learn the beliefs of their teachers, of their friends or society. In fact, school can be an opportunity to escape family beliefs or even open the doors to a new conditioning, more standardized, more focused on intelligence and knowledge but as cumbersome as the others.

Exercise
Look for your beliefs coming from school, a professor, a teacher or school friends.

3. Because we need to fit in and be popular

Teenagers absorb a lot of beliefs. They try to become someone, to become what is expected of them and yet they try to be original. To do it all, they absorb beliefs of their friends and opinion leaders who seem cool to them. Teenagers are easily going to adopt the beliefs of a celebrity: an actor, a singer... They will also adopt the beliefs of their friends so they can feel part of the group. Teenagers are fragile, they try to be nonconformists with their parents and therefore they conform to other beliefs.

Exercise

Search beliefs that come from your teenage years and try to find who passed them onto you.

4. Around the age of 20, in order to fit in socially and professionally, to be "rational"

To become someone, to grow up, to become an adult and be responsible require teenagers to become permeable to beliefs regarding business, work and the world we all consider as "rational". These beliefs are no better than others, but they seem logical, they are taken for granted because many share them.

Saying that we are "rational" does not prove that we have a scientific mind or that we are trying to see the truth as it really is. Usually, people who say they are "rational" often are people who doubt and prefer to keep beliefs they consider "normal », even at the cost of eliminating valuable information from the spectrum of possibilities…

The goal is to become competent, to fit in and be "normal". A lot of our beliefs come from that period of life.

Look at dreams or attitudes you have betrayed when you became an adult. What kind of things seemed rational to give up? Try to find what motivated you to abandon these dreams or attitudes.

5. Through people around you

Beliefs are passed on from one person to another, especially when someone is supposed to have a special knowledge. For example, we believe a mechanic when he gives us his opinion on the quality of a car brand. Similarly, we believe the doctor who talks to us about cholesterol.

We are more likely to resist beliefs from people who don't know as opposed to beliefs from people who are "supposed to know": a dentist, a neighbor, your child's teacher, a lawyer, a mechanic, a plumber, or a painter... When we are not competent in a field, we potentially absorb the beliefs of those who explain how it works to us.

Our friends' beliefs are also contaminating. We love our friends, we respect them, we want to be loved by them, and sometimes we want to be like them. We will absorb their beliefs more easily than others.

6. Through scientific "facts"

When you read a scientific journal, you believe what you read, because it is written in a scientific journal. You are sure of what you claim when you say: "the Big Bang happened 30 billion years ago ». You believe it. You are sure of it. It's proven; it was in a scientific journal. It does not matter whether, a few months later in the same magazine, you have read «that the Big Bang happened 13 billion years ago». You

36

will not change your mind, you know it is true.

Yet scientists know that they know nothing. They can only explain a small part of the world. Newton's physics is valid in a given universe. It responds to specific causalities that are related to our size, our planet and what is perceived by our senses. If you enter the world of the infinitely small, Newtonian physics can be contradicted. The first scientists who have studied the subject, taken aback by new and unpredictable experiences, had to create a new physics, Quantum Physics.

We tend to simplify things and absorb knowledge wrongly and then turn the results into beliefs.

Here is a small selection of scientific beliefs (and / or religious ones) from past centuries to the present day:

    - Women have their periods to "purge themselves of their bad moods" (Hippocrates).
    - The earth is flat.
    - The sun revolves around the earth.
    - The soul is in the heart; the brain is of no use to the body.
    - Homosexuality is against nature.
    - Women should not have children after 30 years old.
    - Diseases are created by malignant body fluids that accumulate in the body and must be purged with bleeding.
    - Bleeding is beneficial to all diseases.
    - Black people are less intelligent than white people because they have a smaller brain.

This is a quote from the "Grand dictionnaire universel"

published in 17 volumes by **Pierre Larousse** between 1864 and 1890.

Grand Larousse (quote on Tobacco, Volume XIV): "Doctor Demeaux says, since people have started smoking in the Lot Department (France), their general health has improved. How can we make people admit that smoking shortens life, when statistics irrevocably establish that human life has increased in recent times, probably due to another factor, but in line with tobacco consumption".

This quote shows how statistics can be misinterpreted.

7. Through religious and New Age movements

Religion is an obvious source of beliefs. You've probably already thought about it. And I will not dwell on the subject. But it is interesting to note that in today's society where religions are in decline, a movement more popular and open attempts to bring religion to another level. Thus the religious are trying to finally overcome the old dogmas to bring their faith more directly to the believers. This movement is explained by some abandonment of beliefs that no longer correspond to our way of thinking.

Obviously, all religious beliefs are included in moral and hereditary beliefs. They are part of our "common sense" even if a person is an atheist.

The New Age movement is a new source of beliefs, often a mix of Hindu, Buddhist, Christian, Gnostic, American Indian and South American beliefs. It is mixing positive thinking and religion, beliefs about signs, numbers, and rituals. It exhumes old shamanic practices or Egyptian traditions. Some turn to old traditions because they are searching for a better world and for a meaning, but is it a good idea?

8. Through the media (TV, Radio, Newspapers, Books, Internet)

The media are spreading as many beliefs as they are spreading facts. Their judgments about facts they relay or people they interview are bearing a lot of their personal beliefs. If all the media programmed the same interview, then this point of view would become a sort of reference for the reader, the audience, who can create a belief from it.

Moreover, the angle, the frequency of certain subjects and the way they are approached will force the audience to believe this or that: "Crime is increasing," "People have no more respect", "when I was young, the world was not so hard", "Foreigners are the worst criminals" ...

9. Through inheritance

Beliefs can also be inherited.

Perhaps, It is the least obvious from the list but it is also the most important one.

We belong to a family. It has influenced us from the first moments of our lives. We received a whole genetic patrimony from them, which is information encoded in the flesh. It is not so strange to imagine that beliefs, which are information as much as genetic codes, could be passed on at the same time.

This is something I cannot prove in a scientific way, of course, but I was able to see it in my work. When you erase inherited beliefs, something happens: a change, a release that will bring a difference in your life or mind.

THE NEGATIVE INFLUENCE OF BELIEFS

Beliefs influence your actions and decisions

We saw in the chapter called the Nature of beliefs that beliefs influence our thoughts, emotions and actions. This influence is colossal. We just need a small belief to block a lot of things.

Let's look at how beliefs block our freedom of action and decision.

Some beliefs paralyze your actions, because you do not dare to transgress what you believe in.

For example

If you think horse riding is dangerous, you will never try it. What if you were missing something that could fulfill you?

If you believe that owning a dog means too much trouble, you will never take one and you will never know the unconditional love a dog can give you.

If you believe that you are ugly or uninteresting, you will never dare to do something to meet somebody.

If you think you cannot be loved, you will fail to see how much some relatives love you.

On the other hand, if you transgress what you believe in, you may have to pay for it later. It all depends on how powerful other beliefs about transgression and punishment really are and on what you suppose may happen if you break your inner laws.

For example:

You believe that you always forget something before going on a trip, but for once, instead of checking everything three times, you try to be more spontaneous and only check things twice. Then "bang", at the airport, you realize that you forgot the pacifier for your baby or her/his lunch maybe. Disaster, of course! Your beliefs about how bad it is to be spontaneous and unprepared coupled with the belief that "you always forget something if you don't check three times" have validated their programming ...

They change the course of your life

First we must consider that we are the ones creating our lives. To understand this, I propose a little exercise:

If you were to rate your current life as a percentage — where 100% means that your life is ideal, without any failure, any unpleasant compromises and where all your dreams come true — how would you rate your life now?

Now, turn this percentage into a score from 0 to 10 (i.e., 70% would become 7). This score from 0 to 10 is what we may call your life creation. Record this number somewhere, as a reference.

If you scored above 6, it obviously means that your life is pleasant enough. You live a life where you feel in control of what happens to you. Generally speaking, you have the life you want, even though you do not have everything you want. You will tend to believe that life is positive and that things tend to turn to your favor. Is this right?

If you scored 5 or below, life may seem difficult, unpleasant, sad, hard or boring maybe. It may be in perpetual opposition to what you want and desire.

Exercise

Try to step back and this time, score your childhood and your teenage years. Use the same method. Compare these grades with your life creation one. What do you see? An improvement? Deterioration? Similar scores?

To put things in perspective, try to grade your father and mother's life creations. Use everything you know about them to find out what their score would be. You will not be objective obviously but nevertheless it can be interesting to do and make you understand where you come from.

I often ask my students and patients to give me an idea of their ability to create their lives by asking such questions. Those questions put things in perspective and it is what we will try to work out in this book. We will try to improve your ability to create your life while helping you erasing your beliefs. In fact these two things go together.

By scoring life creation, I noticed that the majority of my students are in the middle category, 10 to 20% are above and 20-30% below.

Let's look at the following categories:

- The "middle class" (5-7)
- The "poor" (0-4)

- The "rich" (8-10)

Intentionally, I opted for the standard social categories, because it fits well with the idea of life creation. We can generalize and conclude that rich people have a better life creation than poor people. That does not mean they are happy but that they are more likely to obtain what they want in life. Obviously this is a recurrence and not an absolute truth.

This statistic suggests that this could be formulated in one sentence:

"We tend to create what we wish for."

I invite you to consider this possibility but not to believe in it.

Exercise

Say this sentence aloud: "I create my life". Listen to yourself. Repeat it several times to hear yourself, then ask yourself if it is TRUE or FALSE. If this is TRUE, grade how this sentence feels for you from 1 to 10, depending on how strong it is for you in your life. FALSE is 0.

Then say this sentence out loud: "I create my life the way I want." Again, try to hear if it is true or false and note the result as previously.

If you have trouble feeling the difference between right and wrong, true or false, do the following exercise:

Exercise

Say aloud things really false like "I'm a washing machine, I'm a coffee pot, I'm a pen, I'm a chair ..." and try to feel how false it is for your body, for your mind. Memorize this feeling. Pay attention to everything that occurs. Then say sentences that are true for you, such as "I'm a human being, I'm a man/woman, I'm a teacher, a mechanic, a famous astrophysicist, a housewife, whatever it is..." You could of course be surprised by the results but in general you should be able to feel the difference between TRUE and FALSE.

Note that you can grade how true a statement is for you. You can also feel that a statement is FALSE and TRUE at the same time. This means it is a little TRUE.

Having done the exercise above, you should now be able to pronounce the sentence:

"I create what I want ».

And decide if it is true or false for you and if it's true, how true it is from 1 to 10.

As I work with this statement every day with people who can't say it's true, my experience could help you unlock more «I create what I want» in your life.

Do we create our lives?

It's not that foolish to state that we create our lives. In a very pragmatic way, it is evidently obvious that our actions affect our lives.

And who else would create it, if not you? God? Your neighbor?

But some parts of our creation seem very obscure to us. "Why do I suffer? Why am I not successful? Why can't I have children? Why am I constantly feeling in pain? Why oh why is this happening to me when I do not want this to happen in my life?"

All those "why" which we cannot find any answer for, make us doubt about our powerful creative skills.

The most popular response to those questions is the divine will. This excuse has been used so many times over the centuries that it has, in my opinion, lost any meaning. It has become too much of a commonplace. Currently, another excuse is preferred: "it's because you do not believe enough in what you want or because you do not believe enough in yourself ». This is a very dangerous variation.

My simple answer to this question is rather:

> **We create what we want to create at a conscious level but also at an unconscious level. These two states of our being are creating things in our life. Our unconscious mind contains things beyond us, things from our past, from our ancestors and more. Our unconscious mind contains all beliefs we have and these beliefs themselves create without asking our permission, because we have previously validated them within us.**

We have already validated these beliefs. During our childhood, teenage years and finally as an adult we have validated beliefs and accepted them. By wishing to have beliefs, accepting them within us, defending them and then applying them unconsciously to our everyday lives, we open the door to an autonomous creation system in which we loose the control of.

Something is creating in the background, and we are oblivious to it.

Our beliefs are pushing, limiting, blocking or destroying our lives. And they are not the only things creating within us. But as this book is about beliefs, we will focus on them.

A belief is similar to a disease.
It is an embedded need within us but it is possible to get rid of it.
The only problem is our need to believe.

> *NB: Commonly, believing means believing in God. I would not dare to say that this is a disease, but there is indeed a problem of vocabulary here. Replacing "believing in God" with "I would like to think that God exists or I have faith that God exists" and there is no problem anymore. Because in the end, it comes to just that: a need, a desire, an inner confidence and sometimes a mystical experience we have had. Thus, it is possible to be a Christian, a Muslim, a Buddhist or a Hindu without having any beliefs...*

HOW MANY BELIEFS DO YOU HAVE?

This question is key.

Assuming that every belief is a sentence or a statement, in your opinion, how many do you think you have? What is the magnitude of the belief system of an adult?

Over 10? Over a 100? More than a 1'000? More than 10'000?

In fact, it is rather difficult to prove anything in this field. However it seems useful to give you an idea of the magnitude of the phenomenon so that you can appreciate the task ahead of you. From my own experience, whilst working on this, I think we should look at numbers in the range of:

100'000 to 200'000 beliefs

Shocking, isn't it.
Actually it's probably more, given the number of topic in our lives.

CONCLUSION

Beliefs generate conflict. In general, we try to uphold and enforce the beliefs we have. This makes us feel secure and it makes us feel good. This makes us feel important and valued. But beliefs do not fill us with love, joy or peace. They do not allow us to create the ideal life we dream of. They do not allow us to heal. They lock us in a closed thought system and a closed life.

Beliefs make us feel limited and deprived. When we believe something is impossible, we make it impossible to realize. When we believe that we are missing something, we make this feeling exist. Most of us have felt or are feeling deprived and limited, but are these feelings necessary? In absolute terms, is it normal? Is human life like this because we all co-create these standards by believing in them?

Beliefs direct our lives towards obligations where flexibility doesn't exist. Beliefs impose themselves as tyrants. The pain we feel when we see our life going in a direction we don't want is directly related to beliefs.

Beliefs generate much of human beings suffering, and to be able to see it, you can try to understand why you refuse some things or some ideas in your life:

For example:

I cannot tell my boss that I cannot stand him/her. I work too much but he doesn't see it. The company must grow, we must make every effort to achieve this. But I can't work that hard any longer and I do not want to be fired. They don't want to hear any excuses and I must keep going, I can't give up or they'll fire me. Finally, I tried to hold on for so long as I could. Now I am suffering from burnout. I am a burden, I earn less, my colleagues are overworked because of me and everything goes from bad to worse. Perhaps I should have said something earlier.

I have cancer; I was told I was terminally ill. There is no hope. My neighbor told me about a doctor who might help me. He gives me a false hope as if that could do me any good. I was told I was terminally ill, it's over, and it's the end. Doing anything else is useless. Another acquaintance suggested I'd try another type of therapy. Well, that's ridiculous. All these testimonies of miraculous cures on the Internet are not true. They only take money from honest citizens, nothing more. If my doctor and therefore science say I am at the end, then I am at the end. No need to see a second doctor, I prefer to believe mine. I prefer to die with dignity without trying to look like one of those freaky New Age hippies ...

I cannot have children. It hurts me so much, I cry about it every day. It has been confirmed, but I do not want to adopt as my neighbor told me that adopting was a long and painful ordeal. I have also seen on the Internet, people testifying that this is a real nightmare. Therefore it will be a nightmare for me too. Moreover, we don't know anything about the child we would adopt, we could make a bad choice. We could be given someone who is in trouble later. I cannot take that risk, I must give birth to my own child, I am sure of it. Maybe I'll go somewhere in a private clinic abroad to try one of these new genetic technics. That must work surely. I'll try that, even if it costs a fortune. Never mind my husband who prefers to adopt, I am sure of myself, I'm positive, I feel it'll work, I must ... Finally I found a clinic, which charged us $ 20'000 for the treatment. That didn't work ... My husband left me. He doesn't understand my need to give birth to a child and my refusal to adopt. I feel really alone now.

Stop defending your beliefs. They are not fundamentally true. Stop believing that they are necessary because they are not! Try to question your thought system to properly analyze the situation you are in and find the best options.

HOW TO ERASE YOUR BELIEFS?

11 years ago, when I tried to put my life in order and heal myself, something happened. Several things, actually. A succession of events, simple, useful but not miraculous.

It was not a surprise to me, I was trying to sort myself out for quite a while. I was trying to set myself up as a holistic practitioner and I was looking for solutions to my problems everywhere around me.

I was trying to find myself philosophically speaking. As I was studying Buddhism, I followed a training called the Kalachakra, given by the Dalai Lama in Graz, Austria. To put it simply, it is a training to find peace and liberation within oneself. On this occasion, I had the good fortune to touch His Holiness the Dalai Lama when he entered the room. I suddenly felt relieved. I would not have thought nor imagined possible to feel that kind of relief. Some minutes later, I started to cry, releasing something I could not describe. Even now, I do not know what went away that day. But later, I noticed that, finally I had found the answers, more answers. Something in my conscious mind had opened.

Later that year, I went to visit a famous Brazilian healer with my mother who had cancer. There, I met an American man in a wheelchair with whom I talked for a few minutes. He advised me to read a book: "The Power of Now" by Eckhart Tolle. This book had an incredible effect on me. As I was reading and wondering how to apply its teachings, I suddenly had an idea, an inspiration: *to express, to express what I was living out loud, alone in private, without filtering or limiting my expression with my mind.*

I did this for months on end and I noticed it helped me to be more peaceful, to relax, to evacuate my emotions and to understand who I was. Whilst doing this, I realized that expressing feelings was liberating enough to let go of my problems. However, I also found that some sentences were coming back over and over again when I was expressing. They were statements and beliefs.

I concluded that I needed to do something about it and one evening I had an illumination, a revelation coming to me:

"Erase the belief that you are your mind"

I thought, "Ok, that's easy, good idea!". I erased this. Just after that, my back started to hurt and I had a backache for three days.

It was incredible, I was turned upside down by this reaction. It made me see that erasing things was working. What an idea! Doing something like this never occurred to me before and I had never even considered deleting anything in me before.

Adventurous, I started to delete other beliefs, slowly, one after another.

Seeing how I reacted after deleting beliefs, I finally realized that erasing really worked. I also concluded that the violent reaction I first had was not necessary but had been there to make me see that I was on the right track. Therefore I deleted the belief that a violent response was necessary and I carried on erasing beliefs experiencing fewer reactions and noticing it became easier and easier to do.

Some years later, I started to teach this method. And I noticed that everyone could do it. It was actually a method that could be used by everyone.

WHAT DO YOU GAIN FROM DOING THIS?

When erasing your beliefs, you let life give you <u>its own</u> answers, answers that could sometimes surprise you. Allowing your intuition and your analytical mind to work perfectly without being blocked by any prejudice.

Everyone will face this differently, but from my own experience and the experience of my patients and students, here is a list of what you can gain from erasing your beliefs.

You can change your way of thinking

You can become more objective, you can start being less judgmental, more open, more aware, listen more to others and yourself, be more inspired, less constrained by the thoughts of others and by what society demands. It will also help you bring your thoughts back to the present time and to treat each situation as if it were exceptional. Therefore, you can easily be an inventor, a discoverer, a philosopher, and a free thinker.

You can also keep your mind calmer, more peaceful and be in a position to receive as well as pass information on.

Exercise

Say the following sentences aloud and do the exercise of TRUE-FALSE as taught in chapter " the negative influence of beliefs" and make a note of the results.

- My mind is calm

- I control my mind

- I'm open-minded

The result of this test should tell you the current state of your mind.

You can change your behavior and attitudes

We can have some attitudes, which can be unpleasant: being angry, depressed, pessimistic, fearful, submissive, too controlling, a victim, a tyrant...

These compulsive behaviors or attitudes can be corrected.

You can change how you react emotionally

Many emotions are triggered by our internal beliefs. These emotions are often unpleasant and rarely positive. Some people are constantly "polluted" by their emotions, which they have the greatest difficulty to control. To know how to control ourselves is fundamental in order to live in society. Working to have a better self-control is a valid objective.

Erasing your beliefs can help you soothe yourself and reach a greater emotional calm.

Exercise

Say the following sentences aloud and do the exercise of

TRUE-FALSE, write the results down.

- I control my emotions

- I am the master of my emotions

- I have anger in me

- I'm angry

- I have fear in me

- I have sadness in me

The result of this test speaks for itself. Note that we can be emotional "containers". If you have obtained TRUE at 8 out of 10 for "I have anger in me", it means that you are soaking in some repressed feelings of anger at 80% of your maximum capacity. You can get a very different answer to the phrase "I am angry" because this statement refers to the present time. We can imagine to have a situation where "I am angry" is FALSE, but "I have anger in me" is TRUE and vice versa.

You can become more intuitive and analytical

Beliefs promote ignorance. When we have beliefs, we ask ourselves fewer questions. We do not use our intelligence, consciousness and intuition as much. We have some ready made solutions available for each problem. If you believe that you do not know something, then you do not try to understand it. If you believe that you know the solution, then you are not really looking for the answer. Our beliefs put our intelligence on hold.

If you use both your intuition and your analytical skills together, this can help you in your everyday life to resolve all problems you may encounter and find happiness.

Exercise

Say the following sentences aloud, do the TRUE-FALSE

exercise and write the results down.
- I am intuitive
- I am intelligent
- I cannot know
- I am ignorant

You can cure some things

Working as a holistic practitioner, I often see how erasing beliefs can help someone heal. The interaction between our beliefs and our body is very powerful, and some diseases are caused by negative unconscious beliefs.

Furthermore, your beliefs can sabotage yourself and stop you from calling a doctor, having surgery or going to see a holistic practitioner who could help you.

You can use this method to complement (but not replace!) traditional medicine and other therapies that you can follow.

Exercise
If you are sick, say:
- I can heal
- I have the right to heal
- I must be sick
- I have no alternative but to be sick
Do the TRUE-FALSE exercise to see if you do not sabotage this fundamental point.

You may feel freer and more creative

Erasing your beliefs will make you feel freer and less limited.

Gradually you will accept that doing yourself good and to take care of yourself is all right. You will be able to think and act differently; you will feel immense, boundless. You will have the feeling that you can do things now you thought impossible before. You will feel more creative and you really will be more creative.

Exercise

Say the following sentences aloud, do the TRUE-FALSE exercise and write the results down.

- I'm free

- I feel free

- I can create

This can show you what you may lack of.

You may realize that you belong to yourself

You may not have realized this yet, but in the end, you belong to one person, yourself. You do not belong to your parents, spouse, children or friends. This notion of belonging is essential I think. Indeed, it means that you are your own master. You have the right to change, to evolve, and to modify who you are for your highest good.

Exercise

Say the following sentences aloud, do the TRUE-FALSE exercise and write the results down.

- I belong to myself

- I am my own master

The result of this test speaks for itself.

You can discover the gifts within you

Like me, when proceeding with the cleaning of your beliefs, you could develop some gifts such as being able to listen inside others or seeing things that others do not see.

I do not believe in innate gifts. Certainly, some people have a gift since they were born, however it is also possible to develop one. I'm not talking about developing a mystical and supernatural gift, like superheroes in a film, but to simply stimulate or create a professional, artistic or sensory gift.

Exercise

Say the following sentences aloud, do the TRUE-FALSE exercise and write the results down.

- I am gifted

- I can have gifts

You can open yourself to Consciousness

In the absence of beliefs you will find that your mind starts opening to give you a larger and fuller access to yourself and your unconscious. You will truly see yourself. You will find yourself. Discovering yourself will allow you to open to life more extensively and deeply. In other words, you will open to Consciousness.

However, this will only happen if you are interested in doing so. If this particular aspect of personal development does not interest you, there is no reason for this to happen. But sometimes this gift can be hidden and a small stimulation will let it out.

Exercise

Say the following sentences aloud, do the TRUE-FALSE exercise and write the results down.

- I am conscious

- I know myself

Take this test assuming that you are torn between conscious and unconscious. To be conscious at 6 means that you know 60% of who you are. Repeat this test often. At first, your perception may be overstated. Over time, you will find that numbers are more consistent and reasonable. The more things we discover, the more we realize that we do not know everything. The maximum level of your consciousness may vary depending on your progress.

You can change your life

It is a long process to change our life and make it what we want it to be but this work is really worth it.

When you start erasing your beliefs following the method I will explain in the next pages, you may notice that many things will work out by themselves.

They are often details: emotions subside, your behavior changes, a pain disappears, people react differently around you, you dare saying no to people, you do something that you never dared doing before...

These small details will show you that something is at work even if a difficult problem is not solved.

To really make a difference, you must seize this method and use it every day to delete all the beliefs arising in your mind.

ERASING

How to eliminate our beliefs?

The answer is simple. Just erase them.

You just have to say: "I erase this belief."

"What?"
I can already hear you say! :-)

Yes, it is simple, so simple that it seems impossible, doesn't it.

Yet, it works.

To help you, I am going to try to explain the deletion theory. It's not a scientific proof, just a personal opinion.

Theoretical hypothesis

A. Erasing is a sort of omission.

You delete things from your mind every day without realizing it. You forgot what you ate yesterday, the presents you received for your birthday, and all sorts of details of your everyday life. It's easy to forget happy moments, for example. However, we remember quite well the unfortunate moments of our existence. Erasing will restore a balance to help you return to a more optimistic inner state.

Forgetting is a necessary and healthy function of our being, but the modern human being is often afraid of losing sight of things. "We mustn't forget our keys, to pay our income tax and our bills, to think about our mother, to do this or that..." We are increasingly trying not to forget anything because we fear to lose sight of some details that matter. This is not about forgetting the practical details of our daily life, however it's about losing sight of painful sufferings we have experienced. Forgetting is a good way to heal.

<u>Erasing is forgetting voluntarily</u>. This is "making some muscles, we seldom use, work again". It's not that complicated.

B. In a more metaphysical sense, erasing is similar to "un-creating".

For example
To create — — —>
To "un-create" (to erase) <— — —

If the Big Bang were a rough description of what the Creation is, erasing would be the contrary. That is to say to send something tangible back to an empty space full of potential (vacuity).

We constantly use the process of creating to go in one direction to create thoughts, money, problems, emotions, energy, works of art, houses, jobs, ...

We probably also use the "un-creation" process but we do it unconsciously.

The "un-creating" conscious can simplify our lives. It brings a kind of balance.

Imagine that a belief is a subatomic particle and not only a concept or an idea. "Un-creating" would then be the process of removing an infinitesimal unit of information e.g. as small as a sequence of 1 and 0 used in computer programming.

The Method

The engine used to erase a belief is the intention, the desire. I am not asking you to dance around a table with a candle on the head. In other words the vital part is not the how you do it but it is your intention, your desire to delete your beliefs. You must also be focused and aware when you do it.

The most reassuring way to proceed is to speak aloud.

> *For example*
> *Say this out loud: "I clear the belief that it is impossible to erase things."*

Doing this aloud will give this process a greater strength. For now it is a necessary foundation to rest on, later on you will be able to erase without it.

I now invite you to read and delete the beliefs that are listed below. These are the most frequent arguments I found using this method of working. This will unlock your ability to erase.

"Erasing things is impossible, a belief does not disappear just like that!"

It depends on the strength of a particular belief, and why we have it. It depends on how much you resist the process of erasing that belief. But as soon as you want it to work, it happens. If you do not try to do it, you will never know what is behind the mirror.

If you do the exercise hoping that it won't work, to prove that it does not work, then do not be surprised if it doesn't work. ;-)

Beliefs
- Erasing is impossible.
- A belief cannot be deleted.
- Erasing does not work.

"Erasing is far too easy!"

OK, so why is that? Who said that life or change should be complicated. Isn't that also a belief?

Why do you agree with this complexity? Is it because our education system gives us complex trainings? Is it because you believe that acquiring knowledge is not easy? Is it a personal sense of being powerless? Think about your objection, does it come from some beliefs and memories you have or personal experiences you lived? Therefore, what is the real value of your objection? If you find out that there is no real evidence supporting your objection, it just disappears by itself.

Beliefs

- Life is complicated.
- Only complicated methods really work.
- Something simple doesn't work.
- Only smart people can succeed.
- The more complicated the method the more likely it is to succeed.

"Why not just change our beliefs?"

Because changing beliefs means replacing them by other beliefs. This means that there are some good and bad beliefs. That is not the case. All beliefs are bad because they bring about the creation of a limited reality and way of thinking. Furthermore, methods to change beliefs already exist but this is not the purpose of this book.

Beliefs
- There are good and bad beliefs.
- Erasing good beliefs would be terrible, I must not do this.
- Good beliefs help us in life.

"If I erase my beliefs, I take the risk to change who I am and what defines me as a person."

From my experience this is not what happens. I draw this from my own experience coupled with the experience of hundreds of patients I have treated and of students who attended my courses. The reason is simple: our true identity isn't built upon our beliefs. It is modified by these, however it exists in itself. Every choice we made, every memory we recorded gives us a meaning and a definition of a Self. Beliefs alter this definition and they actually keep us from seeing who we are but they are not essential to the existence of a Self.

Beliefs
- Our beliefs build our identity.
- Our being, our spirit and our body cannot exist without beliefs.

"But if I delete a belief, how can I tell it won't come back?"

You are an anxious person, aren't you? You truly think that you are missing something in the creation process or in your body. You think that you are not in control. I understand, I was anxious as well. But do not worry, anxiety or fear cannot defeat the deletion process. When we erase we use our intention, our desire, which means taking the decision to do it. As soon as you pronounce the words you start erasing and there is no turning back. However, you can get this belief back through transmissions or because once more, you live the experience making you believe that. And sometimes you just want to recreate it. But it does not matter, you can erase the belief again.

Beliefs
- Erasing does not work.
- No matter what I do, it never works.
- I do not control anything.
- Beliefs will come back.

If you continue reading, you will see that you can erase beliefs faster than you can recreate them. Therefore, after a while, your system will let go and you will stop creating new beliefs. But if you resist, this can actually take time. You will need to be patient.

"I can't do it."

It's a belief. Consider erasing this first.

> *Belief*
> *- I can't erase my beliefs, I won't manage it, and it's not possible.*

"I do not have the right to delete my beliefs, surely God gave them to me. "

You're the one saying this but when you started reading this book, you probably didn't know you had beliefs. Or maybe you don't see beliefs as I do. Please do not confuse faith with beliefs. You can have faith in God, Allah, Jehovah or Buddha and keep this faith.

I do not find contradictory to have faith in a God and erasing beliefs...

> *Beliefs*
> *- God wants us to have beliefs.*
> *- To have beliefs and to have faith are the same thing.*

"Are beliefs evil, then? "

No, beliefs are just mistakes, internal illusions.

> *Beliefs*
> *- To believe is wrong.*

- To believe is good.

"Is it safe to delete things like that? "

Based on all beliefs I have erased, I would say yes. Everything leads me to think that it is safe to do.

Beliefs
- Erasing is dangerous.
- Erasing is trivial.
- Erasing generates processes.

But sometimes the transformation process, following some deletions, can be difficult to live. Erasing a belief can have physical consequences such as aches and pains, inflammation, exhaustion, increased energy, relief or relaxation. It can also have emotional or mental consequences i.e. joy, euphoria, prostration, depression, emptiness, bad mood, need to be alone...

Once the process has ended, it usually last between a few days and a few weeks, you will go back to your normal but "improved" self. Improved in the sense that the deletion process may have freed you in one or several areas of your life.

If you constantly erase beliefs, the on-going process makes it difficult to see what comes from deleting and what comes from your own life. That's why I recommend taking breaks especially after the global erasing process I will propose later on. You just need to rest for a few days or a week to recover.

If you are emotionally fragile, you may find that the process affects you more than others but this will eventually subside. I suggest you make the corrections at a slower pace, taking a few days between each exercise.

If you have a mental problem (psychosis, schizophrenia, manic depressive disorder...) the deletion process will shake you up too much. I would suggest not trying it out. However if you feel a strong need to use this method, make sure you do it very slowly and surrounded by people who can help you if a problem occurs within days, weeks or months after the correction.

"If erasing were possible, someone would have already found it. "

You have already erased a lot of memories, it means consigning them to oblivion. You also deleted beliefs that were in total contradiction with other beliefs you already had, this is what scientists or psychologists call "filtering". But you did all this unconsciously.

Philosophers have been teaching us that the world is not what it seems. For centuries they have been telling us about beliefs, the problem is that human beings have a peculiar hearing impediment. :-)

Belief
- If it were possible to erase beliefs, someone would have already found it.

Ready now? Let's do it!

Exercise
Try to say which elements of the deletion process you find impossible aloud. Make a note of the sentences coming to your mind and then say the following statements aloud:

"I erase all beliefs that I know or I do not know about erasing, I delete all beliefs stopping me from deleting."
Do you have any other objections? If so, erase them all.
You must keep a neutral view to carry on. Keep an open mind. Be confident. Nothing bad will happen if you just erase sentences, right? So, try it! Your own experience will put this method to the test. Play the game consistently.

There you are, excellent!

Here is how it all starts.

Erasing your first belief is the first step towards many more. All other things you will erase later on will strengthen this move, this flow.

RESISTING

Most people struggle with the idea of changing their beliefs.

It is easy to resist change and access to consciousness. Sometimes, trying to understand is unpleasant. I expect you will have to fight some battles yourself.

On the other hand, you are reading this book, so I assume that you are willing to do it.

To help you, you will find below the various reasons, which could make you hesitate.

Believing is part of our education

We are told: "that's the way it is", "that's the way it works", "you can't have everything" and we obviously believe all this because we try to fit in a "standardized" society.

Going out of our comfort zone

When we start developing ourselves, we lose our child like comfort zone. Children have a low level of consciousness, which make their life comfortable — that is to say they have parents to look after them! Growing up, we must learn to change and to raise our level of consciousness so we can look after ourselves.

Some people refuse to grow up, change and raise their awareness because they are afraid to go out of their comfort zone. Therefore they will depend upon other adults who will need to think on their behalf. They will also do everything they can — consciously and unconsciously — to preserve this dependency (whilst it remains pleasant).

Depending on someone however is a prison and a burden. It's a prison for the adult who refuses to raise his/her level of consciousness and a burden for those who must be aware and act on their behalf.

It's too hard

There are so many beliefs everywhere that you can find some in any of your sentences. They take a big space in your life. You are so immersed in them that you cannot see them anymore. Therefore it is easier to deny their existence than actually address the problem.

It may seem too complicated or impossible to work on your beliefs. For some people it is frightening and they do not feel able to deal with a "mountain". Yet tackling this is not so difficult, you just need to do it methodically and gradually.

I must be right

We are educated to show who we are; to assert our ego and

to think we are right. Whether at home, at school or in the workplace, we always meet people who "are right" and who make sure we know it. So why wouldn't we be right ourselves? Some people will battle with this book just to be right, because they have been formatted to think that way. Others will resist because they feel superior and they do not want to lose that little bit of power they seem to have. When we start our personal development, we need to be humble. Finally for some, personal development <u>seems to be</u> conflicting with their culture or religion.

I'm scared to lose my positive beliefs

Out of all our beliefs, some justify the system itself. We believe that our beliefs are positive or we believe that some are positive and others negative, but that the positive ones are needed.

You need to see beliefs as kidney stones, there are no positive or negative kidney stones, any kidney stone is bad for your health. <u>You believe</u> that some beliefs are positive but that doesn't prove they are! Believing that some of your beliefs are necessary or positive will make you resist or scared to delete them.

In all cases, fear motivates resisting: fear of going out of our comfort zone, fear of the difficulty, fear of not winning anymore or fear of losing something that you think is useful. You must recognize your fears to be able to continue.

Exercise
Now answer honestly to these important questions:
- Are you resisting the speech above? Do you have any objections?

- Do you agree to lose your beliefs?

- What fears have you had while reading this book?

Write your answers down, when you finish this book, check to see if these objections are still valid.

If you want to move forward, delete any belief making you resist the idea of erasing your beliefs.

THE METHOD

To erase your beliefs just be aware that they exist.

The easiest way to erase something is when you have found a statement in your mind.

For example:

If you think life is hard, you say aloud, "I erase this belief."
If you often say that you never have any luck, say aloud "I delete this belief."

It is not necessary to say, "I erase the belief that I never have any luck" but if you prefer you can say it that way. The most important is to keep your mind clear and focused in order to say things decidedly. The "How you say it" doesn't matter, but it's your intention to delete that counts.

You must watch and listen to yourself to discover beliefs you have in you.
Keeping an eye on your actions and on how you anticipate things will also help you see your beliefs.

You could start by taking the beliefs mentioned in this book and delete them one by one. It would be useful to try and feel what physical, emotional and mental impact it has on you. Some people feel when the deletion is done, others don't.

Say it aloud

It is necessary to pronounce sentences aloud. Certainly at the beginning it is.

With practice, you will no longer need to say things out loud. You will just need to think about statements. But take your time before doing this. Erasing is simple but we all need a little ritual to reassure and validate our action. Speaking aloud will help you.

Be aware

The important thing is to be aware, focused and present during the erasing process. Do not think about anything or watch TV at the same time.

With experience you will probably do it so fast that you will be able to do it while watching TV, but this is an advanced course ;-) do not skip stages.

Look for statements

Beliefs are always statements. There is something certain about them. But the types of sentences we use can surprise us. Here are some typical examples:

- *I think that...*
- *That's the way it is...*
- *I know that...*

- *I'm sure that...*
- *I am certain...*
- *It's like that.*
- *I have no doubt that...*
- *I'm convinced that...*
- *It's the truth...*
- *I feel that's how...*
- *I guess...*

Find your beliefs looking at the problems you have

A great way to find our beliefs is to address the problems we have.

For example:

Money is tight, then ask yourself the following question: what are my beliefs about money, the rich, the poor or how to make money? You will easily find a dozen beliefs on this subject. Now imagine having a lot of money, dream about it and watch. Very quickly you will have some ideas and thoughts awakening some fears in you, for example, "if I become rich I will become obnoxious, or "people will be jealous of me", or "I'll get sick..." Beliefs are not necessarily logical, they often are absurd but they are very powerful.

You are always late. What beliefs could cause this situation? If you cannot find any, imagine being on time or early for an appointment and let all negative feelings and prejudices come to you, e.g.: "Arriving early will disturb people, being there at 9am means starting from 9am, it takes me 30 minutes to get there (although in reality it takes 45minutes), I don't know how to be on time, it's not polite to be on time or early, better be a little late... "

Working on groups of beliefs

Beliefs are inter-connected by all sorts of associations. These associations are similar to our memorial associations. We associate a flavor with the memories of a place, with someone's face or an emotional state.

Remember the ice cream you were eating as a child, or eat an ice cream now and look at what it reminds you of. This flavor has the power to make you feel happy, careless, or lighter again (at least if it's a happy memory).

We do the same with all our memories and also with all our beliefs. It is therefore possible to tune into a belief without finding its exact meaning. This is what happens when we try to tune into a specific radio station searching all frequencies.

For example:
You have beliefs about cleanliness. These beliefs depend on your education, your family life and the people with whom you have lived or with whom you live now. Each of us has a very specific understanding of cleanliness and those are based on memories and beliefs we have. You could delete all your beliefs about cleanliness, and then erase beliefs about how to be clean or how to clean your house. This way, your natural ability to combine different elements is used to find and erase dozens of beliefs that would have been very difficult to see otherwise.

In the following chapters we will see how to use context to identify beliefs. This will allow us to work much faster and in a much more systematic way. I invite you to apply immediately what you read, chapter after chapter rather than reading everything and then come back to the exercises. Each exercise will allow you to do the following one. Think of it like a dance class first teaching you simple steps to be able to do more complicated ones later.

Moreover, I think it would be profoundly useless to read this book without making the exercises. To acquire an " intellectual " and theoretical knowledge will not allow you to recognize your beliefs for what they really are. Without the empty space, free of beliefs, created by the deletion process, you will not succeed in recognizing your most limiting beliefs or those who are hidden in the depths of your unconscious.

BELIEFS ABOUT BELIEFS

Some fundamental beliefs make you choose to believe and fear the deletion process. You accumulate beliefs because you want to. This is not an obligation. If you realize that beliefs are unnecessary and limiting, you stop creating them and they can disappear spontaneously.

These fundamental beliefs are what I call beliefs about beliefs and we all have some.

For example:
- I think we should believe.
- Beliefs are useful.
- I must believe to make it work.
- To exist, I must believe.
- I must believe in what I do to make it work.
- I am what I believe.
- I must defend my beliefs.
- I must keep my beliefs.
- My beliefs define my identity.
- I need my convictions, my beliefs.
- I need my beliefs to create things.
- There are good and bad beliefs.
- Without beliefs there's anarchy.

- Beliefs allow us to know what is right or wrong.
- There is no moral without beliefs.
- Beliefs are powerful.
- To believe is to have faith.
- To believe is to trust.
- I must accumulate assumptions, knowledge, beliefs, convictions, opinions and truths.
- I cannot help having beliefs.

Erasing what drives you to constantly create new beliefs would be a huge step forward.

Exercise
Say the following out loud:
"I erase all beliefs I have about beliefs, I erase my conception of beliefs. "
It is an act, a decision, an intention. The word conception is useful to describe a set of beliefs.
Then erase each belief listed above.

Done. Very good! Sometimes after erasing certain beliefs you will feel better. You will feel relieved. You may even sigh. That's a good sign.

Sometimes you will even feel a great inner freedom, a sense of lightness. It may happen with the following exercises. Sometimes you will feel discomfort, resistance, this means that you resist or that you prevent yourself from erasing these beliefs. If you feel uncomfortable be aware of it, try to find out why you are resisting and you will find another belief to erase before you can continue.

INHERITED BELIEFS

I have seen in my work as a holistic practitioner that beliefs are transmitted right at the start of our life, that our parents do not only give us genes as a legacy.

While working on children and babies, I realized that these innocent little creatures already were receptacles of family beliefs.

I do not know how these are passed on. But I reckon it happens during the first three months of pregnancy or even when the baby is conceived. I think the reason why we transmit our beliefs is our urge to transmit our experience to our children. We believe that sharing our experience, our values and opinions is necessary, we want this to happen and therefore it does.

"Family views" are the most common beliefs we share with our descent, but you can also find maxims, superstitions and "advice" on life.

For example:
- *Life is hard.*
- *You never get something for nothing.*
- *Better say nothing than nothing to the purpose.*
- *A child must be seen but not heard.*

- *The world is getting worse.*
- *We must hide our emotions.*
- *Our family is unlucky.*
- *I'm not beautiful.*
- *Better be intelligent than beautiful.*
- *Money only brings worries.*
- *Love hurts.*
- *Life is unfair.*
- *Success is hard work.*
- *I must fall in love with someone similar to me.*
- *Better keep our secrets.*
- *Better not change anything.*
- *A bird in the hand is better than two in the bush.*

You don't have to keep these beliefs to stay true to your family or to be like your parents. Your need to belong can sabotage your intention to delete. The important thing is to love your family not to be like them. Only beliefs require you to be like your family, you don't need to be.

Are you ready? Have you erased the beliefs preventing you from doing this? Let's go!

Exercise
Being very focused, say the following out loud:
"I erase all my inherited beliefs. "

You just done it!

How do you feel?

Some people feel this correction very strongly. Doing this means erasing nearly a quarter of our beliefs! This is not a trivial deletion process!

CORE / FUNDAMENTAL BELIEFS

I noticed that some beliefs are even deeper rooted than inherited ones. They may come from a common background all human beings have, they could come from previous lives if you believe in that (ha! We need to use that word carefully...).

All I know is that these beliefs are present in every one of us and "fundamentally" contributes to our unhappiness.

For example:
- Life is hard.
- I must suffer to get what I want.
- We're always alone.
- Life is complicated.
- Death is the worse thing happening to us in life.
- We must be afraid of death.
- Suffering is unfair.
- I must suffer to evolve.
- I must walk all over other people to be happy myself.

Exercise
Now erase all of your core / fundamental beliefs.
Go on. "Fundamental" does not mean good or useful.

Now that you have erased your core beliefs, you have cleaned the base of your pyramid.

THE PYRAMID OF BELIEFS

We can look at beliefs focusing on the order in which we created or received them to build a kind of pyramid. This pyramid shows how robust belief systems are.

The chronological deletion process helps put things into a time context. Your thoughts are focused on the chronological aspect of your beliefs. Therefore they can easily understand which beliefs belong to them, hence the global deletion process' efficiency.

Here is the pyramid of beliefs as I see it:

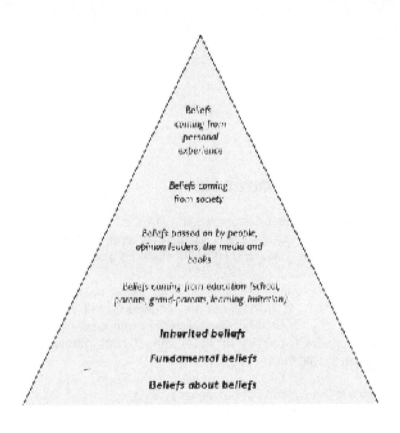

Beliefs coming from personal experience

Beliefs coming from society

Beliefs passed on by people, opinion leaders, the media and books

Beliefs coming from education (school, parents, grand-parents, learning, initiation)

Inherited beliefs

Fundamental beliefs

Beliefs about beliefs

You just cleaned the base of the pyramid, which maintains cohesion and keeps a strong belief system. Erasing the base first easily breaks the system.

You can pause here if you wish to have time to feel how these deletions impact on you. Just a reminder, deleting happens instantly however each deletion has a process. Just accept this process and see what it brings in you, what it reveals. Deleting often brings about a higher awareness and it can be a way to remember things we have forgotten.

TYPES OF BELIEFS

I am about to complicate things a little to take into account the diversity of our language and of our mental structures.

We have seen that a belief is an affirmative sentence.

However, when you say, "I erase this belief", you use a specific word which is not quite the same as "I erase this certainty" or "I erase this conviction". Therefore, the method is not quite complete.

I have realized this during my research. We must take into account the complexity and rich diversity of our language.

In English, I found 7 major categories of beliefs:

- Assumptions
- Prejudices
- Beliefs
- Certainties
- Knowledge
- Truths
- Convictions

An assumption will be stated as "It seems that... I feel that... I'm pretty sure that..." it's how a belief begins.

A prejudice is a kind of assumption, e.g. : "foreigners cheat", we are condescending and we express our contempt in prejudice.

A belief: "I believe that...", "It's like that", "that's the way it is".

A certainty: "I'm sure that... I'm certain."

Certainties simply come from the frequency of recurrences. We create or accept many certainties at work. Willing people and people who are sure of themselves create a lot of certainties.

Knowledge: "I know that's the way it is, I just know it."

Knowledge is a scientific belief. Or it is a belief that permeates society so much that everyone has it and it is impossible to question it. In fact when you say, "I know", you challenge others. You want them to say the contrary because you believe you can prove it.

A truth: "it is the truth, that's the way it is, there is no doubt about it, that's what everyone thinks."

A truth is so well known that it cannot be questioned. Truths are often religious, moral or linked to a personal experience we have lived many times.

A conviction: "I am convinced that, it is my conviction."

A conviction is the pinnacle of a belief. There is probably nothing stronger. We can also talk of absolute certainty.

I have introduced these types of beliefs in a specific order, from the weakest to the strongest. Moreover, in each category, you can grade every belief you find from 1 to 10.

What I noticed is that a conviction is built gradually. We start by making an assumption, and then creating a belief, which finally becomes a conviction...

Therefore, all these types of beliefs exist simultaneously. You can imagine them being a succession of plastic sheets, increasingly thicker surrounding and protecting a personal opinion.

For example:

"Broccoli is good against cancer" is, first of all, knowledge (a scientific fact from a statistical study but it is still relatively factual). You read this in the paper. You may have read, "We can assume, given the statistical studies carried out, that broccoli increases our body's resistance against cancer". The statement is somehow conservative. But deep down you need this to be true and therefore transforms it into knowledge, a certainty, a truth and a conviction. The more you will hear about it, the more convinced you would be. Erasing these beliefs will make you stop thinking that's true. You could still be of the opinion that broccoli can be useful without being fundamental.

So, what is the best thing to do?

When erasing, you will now use these seven words to obtain a complete result.

For example:

"I erase all my assumptions, prejudices, beliefs, certainties, knowledge, truths and convictions about this matter"
Or

"I erase this assumption, prejudice, belief, certainty, knowledge, truth and conviction. "

It doesn't leave much to space or creativity I know, but from my experience it is necessary.

You will now resume erasing as previously, adding these terms to the deletion process.

Exercise

Erase all assumptions, prejudices, beliefs, certainties, knowledge, truths and convictions you have about assumptions, prejudices, beliefs, certainties, knowledge, truths and convictions. (I know it's not light :-))

Delete all your inherited assumptions, prejudices, beliefs, certainties, knowledge, truths and convictions.

Delete all your core/fundamental assumptions, prejudices, beliefs, certainties, knowledge, truths and convictions.

Shortcut

Once you get used to these terms and you have made a certain number of deletions, you can use the term **"conception"** to replace those seven words. It will be more practical and faster to say. But first you must get used to saying the seven words.

For example:

I erase all my inherited and fundamental conceptions.

Again, you can make a break here if you wish to. Leave yourself time to feel what occurs in you. If you do not feel anything special after a few days, you can probably do this at a faster pace.

BELIEFS COMING FROM OUR EDUCATION

At each stage of your development people taught you how they viewed the world. First your parents and your family, then other children, siblings, friends from your day-care centre or school.

You also had adults around you who were responsible for your education (child minders, teachers, professors).

You needed to learn and to fit into society therefore you accepted most of these beliefs without resistance.

Exercise

Now erase all assumptions, prejudices, beliefs, certainties, knowledge, truths and convictions received from your education.

BELIEFS FROM THE MEDIA AND OPINION LEADERS

Growing up, your "innocence" disappeared gradually and you became more suspicious and resisting more to the beliefs of others. But then you have been caught in another type of influence: friends, opinion leaders and the media.

An opinion leader is someone who should know things, someone who shines. It could be a teacher when you were a student, a classmate or a singer from your teenage years.

When we want to look like someone, we absorb the beliefs of that person or create beliefs from what we know of this person.

For example:

If you admired Michael Jackson and wanted to be like him, to be successful you may have thought that you had to be thin, just as he was. If you thought you had to live a similar life to his to resemble him, then you may have tried to change your life to follow his path. Everything he would have said on television could have become gospel for you; all his ideas might have become beliefs.

Exercise

Look at the person you wanted to identify with in the past and look at the beliefs you acquired or created.

The media are an obvious channel to spread an impressive number of beliefs, understandably so, as they sell information and information means potential beliefs.

Consider the media at large: books, newspapers, magazines, news stories, TV shows, movies, series, talk shows, blogs, and all web pages.

Because journalists are supposed to give their opinions or relay the opinions of people they interview, they tend to convey beliefs in their manuscripts without realizing it. It's the same problem as before.

Writers also have that tendency. TV presenters do it as well.

Every single day, the media disseminate a frightening amount of beliefs.

Exercise
Now erase all assumptions, prejudices, beliefs, certainties, knowledge, truths and convictions received from the media at large, opinion leaders and friends.

BELIEFS COMING FROM OUR SOCIETY

More subtle, this category includes all beliefs you may have received from people in general and all standard behaviors we spend years learning.

Erasing these beliefs will complete the two previous deletions.

Exercise

Now erase all assumptions, prejudices, beliefs, certainties, knowledge, truths and convictions received from society and people in general.

BELIEFS COMING FROM YOUR EXPERIENCE

Beliefs you care more about are beliefs from your personal experience, but they are built on beliefs passed onto you. If no one had passed their belief system onto you, you wouldn't create any yourself.

Gradually, as you experience life, you create within you an impressive catalogue of memories and beliefs. You cannot stop yourself from doing this, it happens spontaneously. Each new experience is built on what you have already experienced and what you already believe in. This gives you a sense of continuity and consistency.

It is very difficult for children to challenge this consistency status. They are not conscious enough to be able to do this (at least the majority of children). Teenagers and adults, on the contrary, are more aware and able to question this internal coherence.

However, we are often reluctant to do so. We confuse our identity with this consistency. We tend to protect our identity even if we are not exactly aware of what it is.

In fact, this coherence is not your identity. It's just what you know about yourself at the present time. Changing this coherence will help you change the image you have of yourself without changing the essential or deep nature of your being.

In general, beliefs coming from your experience are resisting the most to the erasing process. That's the reason why I suggest you simply delete these beliefs one by one, as and when they come to mind during the following years. If you are more adventurous and determined you can also do the following optional exercise.

Optional exercise:

Erase all assumptions, prejudices, beliefs, certainties, knowledge, truths and convictions coming from your personal experience.

This deletion may not be as efficient as others and you may need to erase beliefs coming from your personal experience at a later stage. Do not see this as a failure, as I explained, we are particularly attached to these beliefs.

You have now completely erased beliefs from your pyramid of beliefs:

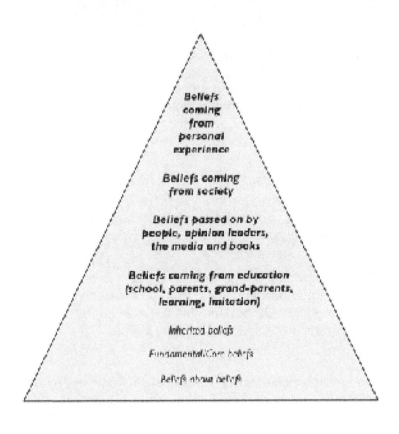

Beliefs
coming
from
personal
experience

Beliefs coming
from society

Beliefs passed on by
people, opinion leaders,
the media and books

Beliefs coming from education
(school, parents, grand-parents,
learning, imitation)

Inherited beliefs

Fundamental/Core beliefs

Beliefs about beliefs

How do you feel?
What experience have you done?
Are you different?
Do you feel different?

Generally I come across three types of reactions after these deletions: feeling better, nothing special and strange emotional or physical reactions.

In all three cases, the correction worked. And remember, you do not need to believe in it to make it work (that would beat everything!).

If you feel all right, you can carry on reading immediately. Otherwise let the process progress and start reading the reminder of the book later. It's not uncommon for the process to take between 3 to 6 months. Some patience is required.

GROUPS OF BELIEFS

Now that we have seen how to erase beliefs in chronological order, we will focus on beliefs we catalogue differently within us.

At the time we create or receive a belief, we link it to something: the object it describes, a person who transmitted it or an event we experienced.

The previous deletion process has very likely succeeded. However, it is also likely that many beliefs are resisting the process. Or to be more precise, some unconscious parts of you are resisting the global deletion process.

To overcome this difficulty, I propose you delete groups or categories of beliefs.

When beliefs are linked to the same subject, they make a category.

For example:
All your beliefs about love are beliefs that are based on your love life, on how to love or be loved. This also includes all beliefs such as: "I am not loved". These are all beliefs influencing or altering your experience of love.

Below you will find a partial list of categories of beliefs. These are only examples. It is obviously possible to find some others. Be creative!

You can delete one category of beliefs at a time, and wait to see what happens. Or you can try to delete several categories in a row to go faster. You can also delete all of these beliefs in 10 minutes as I do when I deliver my training.

Instructions

Choose a category below.

For example:

Consider the category: learning.

Say the following aloud: "I erase all of my conceptions (or assumptions, prejudices, beliefs, certainties, knowledge, truths and convictions) about learning, about how to learn, about how to teach, I erase all conceptions preventing me from learning. "

Repeat the above for each category, varying the sentence accordingly. Follow your intuition. Find your own way of saying things but remember that the way our language is constructed determines our own logical way to proceed. Details matter, if you say, "I erase all my beliefs about learning", it's not the same as saying, "I erase all beliefs stopping me from learning". We are all stuck in different ways, even if we have similar problems.

Categories of beliefs

1. Negatively stated beliefs

I put all negatively worded beliefs in that category.

For example:

"It doesn't exist, it's not possible, it will not work, I do not believe it, I'm not good enough, healing is impossible, change is impossible, women can't do men's work, God does not exist, I can't learn chinese..."

The key is in the formulation and not in the subject matter. You just need to eliminate all your beliefs causing you to always see the problem instead of the solution. These beliefs will generally prevent you from doing things, daring to do things and setting yourself free.

This is one of the corrections you should do first.

2. Creation of the world, the universe, human beings

Religious and scientific beliefs can be found in this category. Erasing these beliefs will help you find your way differently, to find your own path rather than the way your ancestors have made for you. If you are a scientist or a philosopher it may allow you to find new ideas in your field.

3. Your life creation

Beliefs on the subject determine how we see life. Do we have a destiny or not? Do we have the choice or not. Who creates in life? How do we create? What creates in us? Etc.

4. Dreams / Desires / Intentions / Needs

The beliefs you have about your dreams are changing the

way you dream, either during your sleep at night or during the day when you dream of a better life. The beliefs you have about your desires change the way you desire something or let yourself desire something.

For example:

For Buddhists, desire is a force of attachment that is dangerous and indirectly causes Karma and Samsara. Therefore it is best to gradually leave desires behind to access Dharma and Nirvana (i.e. the absence of any suffering and the ultimate enlightenment). Taking it literally, to try not to desire anything, we can block our desire. But the Buddha himself had first desired to relieve all beings from suffering! Wasn't this desire at the heart of his discovery at that time? And after that he had the desire to teach what he found. How can these 2 desires be harmful?

Most of the time, when we think of the word desire, we think of it as sexual or as wanting something superficial and without any value. This conception is, in my opinion, detrimental. To overcome this problem, we use the word "intent" instead to talk about a "healthy" and "fair" desire.

All of this comes from our beliefs about needs. We identified that in our language a need is something fundamental and a desire is something superfluous. A human being who satisfies all of his desires takes advantage, but someone who satisfies his needs doesn't. Looking at things this way is very limiting.

Exercise

Try to erase all your conceptions about these four concepts and erase everything preventing you from dreaming or desiring things. Erase beliefs that desires are less important and necessary than needs are.

Whilst doing this, I have discovered that needs do not exist. The word need only describes a craving: a desire we haven't been able to satisfy or we didn't want to satisfy.

For example:

I want (desire) to drink some water but I don't do it, I ignore this desire. After a while, I am thirsty, my body expresses a need (lack) using a stronger signal. Again we may decide to ignore the signal. After a while, the desire is so strong that it will force us to drink, creating a "vital" need.

The difference we make between needs, basic needs and desires, in our language, is a way to manage what we lack of but it's not a good way to create a great life.

Ignoring a desire for too long will drive us to create a need and this need will become compulsive and out of control. It is better to satisfy desires when they are small, manageable and healthy rather than having cravings.

For example:

Smokers, for example, are eaten away by a compulsive and harmful need. What are they missing in their life to drive them to do that? What are the beliefs pushing them to do that? What kind of need or desire did they deny and if satisfied would allow them to stop that habit?

There are obviously many other harmful desires: violence, drugs, and alcohol...

It is possible to some extent to break free from a need or a desire by erasing some negative beliefs. Doing this is necessary, because it will allow you to have more confidence in your desires. To trust ourselves is easy if our desires are legitimate and respect morality.

Be careful, this is not a miraculous recipe. I am just saying it is possible in some cases. When we have a detrimental desire, it always comes from something deeper, generally inherited beliefs or hurtful experiences during childhood. Erasing your beliefs will not stop all your addictions but it may help you control yourself better or even cure yourself.

Exercise

You can work on your addictions by agreeing to give yourself a better life AND erasing everything that drives you to be addicted.

Lacking something is a repetitive scheme created by beliefs. To complete this work, you can erase your conception of loss and all conceptions generating shortfalls within yourself and in your life.

5. Power / Influence

First and foremost, power is a measure of the desire and the creation capacity of a person. A lot of people are afraid of power, or are afraid to influence others, because every day we see power being used wrongly. However, blocking our creative power or our influence by fear of tumbling down is a good way to sabotage our whole life.

Consider this: "Is it really possible to influence anyone? Not influencing is another way of influencing, isn't it? In this case, is it really relevant to block this strength within you? How is this blockage impacting you? Does it make your life more complicated? Are you too submissive? "

6. Meaning / Impressions / Perceptions

Our senses can deceive us. We know this thanks to science. Our beliefs will often have that same effect on our senses. If intellectually something is impossible, it doesn't exist in our mind and our senses will betray us. Therefore, it's easy to miss some life experiences.

7. God / Life / Source / Connect to God

Erasing your beliefs about God allows you to find God differently. God is similar to a scientific fact. If you delete your belief about God, He doesn't cease to exist!

The problem is mostly what you expect of God, what you think He should do for you. These beliefs may cause you to live a religious crisis.

With the development of New Age, I often hear: "I believe in the Source but not in God". This poses a fundamental problem: if you have a problem with God, you have a problem with the Source and your connection to it. Finding any other word, which suits you better, will not help. In order to be more in tune with Life and the Source, it is better to work on your beliefs about God.

Be aware of non-belief, if you say: "I do not believe in God" it is also a belief!

Do not think that I want you to erase something about God. Do not use this excuse to avoid erasing your beliefs. As I said before, to have faith is not a belief, it is a state of mind. I am just trying to enlighten you with regards to small surprises our beliefs can hide.

8. Beliefs about your soul

We believe a lot of things about the soul, e.g. It is immortal, perfect or immaculate. Or we think it doesn't exist.

If we over rate it, we jump to dangerous conclusions. Such as: beliefs come from the mind but not from the soul, the latter cannot have any, it's so perfect! Therefore we set some limits to our mind, we try to control it at all costs.

However, your mind is an aspect of your soul! Or do you think that the soul is only a small part of you and that everything else can be thrown away?

I prefer to use the word Soul in the sense of "Totality of the Being" e.g. who you are as a whole. At least, like this we are not lost in all sorts of logical contradictions. And if we consider the soul from this point of view, every part of you is a piece of your soul. Therefore, the soul has beliefs and creates some as well.

You see, it's just a question of vocabulary and meaning we give to the words.

On the contrary, if you reject the notion of soul, you lose the ability to see that there are things science cannot even explain with its instruments (e.g. emotions), or you refuse the idea that there might be something after death. In short, we reduce, in an arbitrary but not a scientific way, the range of possibilities that an Alpha and an Omega exists because we exclude altogether a possibility of its working hypothesis.

Our beliefs about the soul are very important and it is very useful to erase your conception of the soul or beliefs affecting your soul and preventing you from feeling it and recognizing it.

9. Expression / Words / Arts

Erase conceptions blocking your expression, your words and your artistic talents. Erase your conceptions of these topics to see them differently.

10. Creativity / Talent

Erase your conceptions of creativity and talent.
Erase all conceptions blocking or altering your creativity and talent.
Erase all conceptions making you think that you have no talent or that you cannot find any.

I think you probably understand the concept! I let you continue with the following categories. Be creative!

11. Relationship with oneself

- Self-confidence / confidence in life
- Body / Health
- Food / Diet
- Digestion
- Sleep / Dreams
- Diseases / Healing
- Suffering / Pain
- Separation / Death
- Sex / Roles in sexuality (woman / man)
- Learning / Education / Intelligence
- Letting go / Failing to remember / Memories
- Pure / Not pure / Clean / Dirty
- Forbidden things / Taboos / Inhibition / Resistance / Sabotage

12. Relationships

- Society
- Intimate / social / love relationships
- Children / Education / School / University
- Family / Relatives / Friends
- Foreigners
- Political parties
- Travelling
- Virus / Transmission / Contagion

13. Work and money

- Money / Fortune / Wealth
- Work / Effort
- Organization / Time Management / Time
- Professions / Occupation
- Lotteries
- Social Security
- State / Taxes
- Government
-

14. Relationship with the planet Earth

- The weather / The climate
- What the Earth is
- Pollution / energy
- What is necessary to do or not do for the planet
- Our country
- Other countries

You can adapt this list to your needs, find other categories, so many things could be added, I leave it up to you to explore what comes to your mind.

Below are some additional questions to help you further:

What prevents you from changing your life? Do you feel powerless? Have you resigned yourself to something or a situation?

Exercise
Erase convictions making you feel this way.

Do you avoid confronting others even if it is necessary to change what's wrong in your life?

Exercise
Erase your conceptions of what conflicts, struggles, confrontations and fights are, erase your conceptions about expressing yourself and saying what you feel and think.
Erase everything you believe about free expression.
Erase the belief (certainty, knowledge...) that "saying what I think inevitably leads to a conflict and a dangerous situation."
Erase the belief (certainty...) that I lose systematically every conflict.

Do you have the impression to always live conflicts, struggles and injustice?

Exercise
Erase your conceptions of what conflicts are; erase your conceptions that conflicts and struggles are necessary.

Erase your conceptions about justice, injustice and the fact that we must fight to achieve what we want or to obtain justice.

Do you feel that no one can help you?

Erase these conceptions: "I cannot be helped. Anyway, no one can help me. I have never been helped and I never will be. I've never been helped properly, the help I receive is inadequate or limited ... "

Do you feel alone?

Erase the belief (...) that you are alone.

Erase all conceptions causing you to be alone, pushing you to seek isolation or preventing you from finding a solution to your loneliness.

Erase your conception of loneliness.

Do you find it difficult to heal?

Erase all the conceptions you have about healing in general.

Erase conceptions making you think that you cannot be cured.

Erase the belief (...) that your illness cannot be cured: cancer, diabetes, multiple sclerosis, fibromyalgia, cystic fibrosis, ... All these diseases that currently cannot be cured by modern medicine.

Erase the belief (...) that it takes time to heal, it hurts, or that you must make a special effort for that to happen (i.e.

to be virtuous, just, good, kind, accepting, humble, combative...)

Healing is sometimes very simple, very quick and easy. The more you erase your beliefs about it, the more you will allow this possibility to occur.

Do you resist change?

Yes, probably. Unintentionally, all of us resist, because we love our identity, our way of thinking and seeing the world. We resist because, from an early age, we are educated like this. Resisting, like fighting, is one of our values.

Erase all beliefs (...) making you resist change and your own change.

Consider the idea that in any case every second you are changing. Your cells die and are renewed every second. It is this constant change that allows you to age slowly so you can recognize yourself in the mirror every morning. It is futile to resist change because change is the essence of who you are.

HIDDEN BELIEFS

Sometimes, to control the situation, have a better life or avoid a problem, we can try to hide some things from ourselves. In psychology it's called *repressions*, and it is used to describe memories of traumatic events removed from our conscious mind but present in our unconscious memory.

You can do the same with your beliefs.

There are several ways to describe this mechanism: we hide beliefs we do not like in a corner of our being, we distance ourselves from that package and we try to remove it from our conscious mind. Thus, it seems we have eliminated the problem but I have been able to see that this suppression is not effective.

This process is only used with embarrassing beliefs we prefer to deny but we don't know how to get rid of.

Erasing these beliefs will be very useful.

Exercise
Erase all assumptions, prejudices, beliefs, certainties, knowledge, truths and convictions you have hidden, removed or distanced yourself from.

121

THE "10 CORE VALUES"

Along the years I have worked with my method, I have realized that many problems could be solved if I worked directly on core values.

Core values are the values we can all agree on. There is consensus. These are values that are essential to our lives. They are also consistent and represent deep desires we all have. Our beliefs significantly affect how we live these.

Here are the 10 values I have chosen following numerous discussions I started during my training sessions:

1. *Love*
2. *Happiness*
3. *Freedom*
4. *Pleasure*
5. *Passion*
6. *Joy*
7. *Beauty*
8. *Harmony*
9. *Peace*
10. *Safety*

The order in which they are listed doesn't particularly matter.

If you want to include other values to this list, check that it cannot be connected to one of the 10 values in one way or other. Respect, for example, is an important value in our society but we can link it to Love and Harmony. Indeed, respect depends on our ability to love, our need to live in harmony, and our Conscience (see below).

Exercise

Measure all these values from 1 to 10. Check these values every 3 months to establish a baseline and to see how you progress.

To measure them, say the following aloud: "I am happy". Is it TRUE or FALSE? If its TRUE then measure how true it is (from 1 t 10).

Sentence such as "I am at peace" or "I am safe" are easy to find, but you might find difficult to make a sentence for some other values, so here are my suggestions:

- Love (I feel loved, I love myself — they are two different but complementary aspects of love)
- Pleasure (I am pleased, I feel pleasure, I experience pleasure, my life is pleasant)
- Passion (I'm passionate about something, my life is exciting)
- Beauty (I am beautiful, I feel beautiful)
- Harmony (my life is harmonious, I feel harmonious, I live in harmony)

Working on these core values will allow you to find solutions to many of your problems and bring change in your life.

For example

If you find that your life is too dull and insignificant, it may probably be because you lack passion. But passion is often misunderstood and misjudged. Passion, as opposed to peace, is thought to be very dangerous. Your beliefs about passion will therefore limit your desire, your ability to desire and to create an exciting life or an exciting relationship. A lack of passion can translate itself in many different ways and can affect many areas of life.

If you have money problems, for example, it maybe due to an issue with the value: safety. I have seen that working on the value safety itself, your relationship with money and fortune can gradually change.

We often contrast values one against another: passion versus peace, freedom versus love ... Our beliefs drive these contradictions. We do not have to make a distinction between them. When we believe that we cannot have everything in life, we start haggling. We ask God or life for a value in exchange for another one we have lost. "Give me health, I will give you my job", "give me love and I will give my wealth (safety)". This unnecessary bargaining is harmful in many ways.

Exercise

To unlock these 10 values, first you must erase everything you believe about them. Delete all your conceptions about the values from the list, then all your conceptions about values in general. As and when the deletion process takes effect, your thoughts about these values will change. Slowly, you will find other beliefs to erase. This work will probably take several months, during which it is important to stay alert and conscious.

While working on these values, I realized something

important: these values are more like energies, a power from the universe.

You could imagine receiving these values as pure energy, rather than think of them just as concepts. You could just accept to open yourself to them and agree to receive them within yourself.

Exercise

Do the TRUE/FALSE test to see whether you are open to these energies or not. Do it for each value.

Delete anything preventing you from opening to these energies, accepting them, loving them and giving you the right to receive them. Delete anything preventing you from creating, giving and spreading these energies around you. Erase everything that drives you to shield yourself from them and block them. Erase everything making you resist them. Delete everything justifying your resistance.

Following this exercise, you can do the TRUE-FALSE test to see if you are more open to each of these energies.

Once you have worked on yourself using this method, it will be easy to estimate your progress by measuring the 10 values. You can do this every 3 months and you will have evidence about what this method has brought to you and avoid presumptions. This point is also true for all tests given in this book.

CONSCIOUSNESS

Consciousness is one of the most beautiful qualities we have and it is also a value.

I think that erasing beliefs will help you be more conscious. Why is that? Because beliefs shield our brain. No need to think, we just need to believe.

From the moment you really try to find an answer, you use your Consciousness. Your Consciousness, with a capital C, is somehow your highest inner guide. At least it should be and it could be.

Use the word in its broader sense. To be aware of good and evil doesn't mean being Conscious as I see it. Good and evil are defined by beliefs like other things may be. Consciousness is not a belief. It's a different vibration state. This state is over and above beliefs.

You have probably experienced what being Conscious is. It can be a feeling of peaceful happiness, the impression that all is well, a meditative state, a moment of pure joy when your mental abilities are at their highest.

But you can also *feel complete and open*.

Sometimes becoming more aware is painful but it makes us evolve in a positive way and its positive implications lead us on our path again. This is what you might find searching for Consciousness.

Slowly and steadily, you will become more Conscious. You will have thresholds to cross. As babies we come to this world with a very low consciousness, we are totally depending on others. Growing up, we develop our coordination and mobility, our senses, intelligence, language AND we become more aware of who we and others are. As teenagers we also jump to another level of consciousness. We suddenly have a higher consciousness, which makes us think we understand everything. We "see" things better, we understand things better, we lose some of our illusions (on our parents, society, school, friends...), we want to discover who we are.

As adults we jump again to another level of Consciousness. For some, it happens early in life and others experience it at a later stage.

Each stage of life has a given level of Consciousness. Unfortunately, once we reach adulthood, we stagnate and tend to stop our progress. However, we have many other lines to cross to progress further.

As soon as we stop our development, as we know it, we could really try to develop our Consciousness, which is not limited to knowledge, or intelligence. To be conscious equal to «I know». It is a kind of instantaneous intuition, a comprehensive, systemic and global understanding.

For example
An experienced painter who learnt how to paint a long time ago and who spends his time perfecting it, playing with what he knows, who goes beyond his limits to create a transcending way of painting is a good example of Consciousness.
It transcends what we know and gives us the capability to

go beyond our abilities. Please understand me, a good painter doesn't necessarily have a high Consciousness, this is just an example to show you that experience and familiarity can help us transcend beliefs and knowledge to go beyond what we know to find an answer.

When we become more conscious, we understand that some things are useless or dangerous for others or ourselves. We are better at collaborating with others and we find easier to co-create a pleasant, functional and grown up society. In a sense, Consciousness helps us to have a more moral life. In another way, Consciousness helps us setting ourselves free from a too narrow morality.

Generally, erasing beliefs will allow you to go through different levels of Consciousness. But I will also offer you some exercises to help you accelerate this process if you want to go faster.

Exercise

Say out loud: I am Conscious and do the TRUE-FALSE test. Write down the number measuring the sentence.

Erase your conceptions about being Conscious, what is good and evil, right or wrong, fair and unfair. Erase conceptions blocking your Consciousness. Erase what prevents you from opening yourself to Consciousness.

Erase your conceptions about intuition, intelligence, knowledge, imagination, how you learn, experience, listening, expression, the senses and how to use it all.

Erase your conceptions about ancestors, heritage, life and death, conceiving, birth, how life develops, evolution, transformation, gifts, abilities, creativity, accomplishments, realizing and finalizing things, how life proceeds, God or the Source, what is after or what there was before life.

Beware of what happens subsequently, you may have new ideas; life may offer you new options or new obstacles. There are lessons to be learnt from the process as you live it. You will be able to rise from these moments if you erase other beliefs, which were buried deep down but are now within your reach. Deleting these beliefs will help you make a staggering progress.

To raise Consciousness, we just need to let ourselves be conscious, to have this desire to accept Consciousness and to open ourselves to Consciousness. It sounds very simple and I hope it will be simple for you, but I have seen how these things can be complicated to accomplish.

I have also seen that many people objected to raise their Consciousness. Resisting Consciousness is due, in my opinion, to several elements: first we resist what is new because it scares us, then we want to protect our routine and to stay somewhat unaware — reminding us of our childhood — and finally we may be afraid to discover that we are not as perfect or nice as we think.

Consciousness allows us to see what is true within and around us. You would be surprised how many people refuse to truly see what they really are.

Nevertheless, if you prefer to see the truth, you can continue with the following exercise.

Exercise
Say out loud:
- I let myself be Conscious.
- I wish to be Conscious.
- I want to be Conscious.
- I agree to be Conscious.

- I open myself to Consciousness.
- I agree to jump further into Consciousness.
- I agree to see the Truth.

Check if these sentences sound TRUE or FALSE and if they are TRUE, measure them from 1 to 10. You will probably get some interesting answers.
Then, if you wish, erase all beliefs blocking or limiting these steps. Be attentive and open to what comes up. You may find answers in your dreams, in some books about therapies, in contact with some people or you could simply have a spontaneous inner illumination.

Forcing your Consciousness to develop is meaningless. You must follow the steps in a certain order. It's not always true but it often tends to happen this way.

I tried to move forward at a faster pace myself. I was discovering new things every day, new things to erase, new ideas, and new treatments. I become more and more aware of certain facts in my life. My mind was really excited instead of calming itself down. I was restless, I was working at night, and I felt extremely tired.

After three years, I felt so exhausted that I decided to slow things down and stop the process. Very quickly I felt the results. I gradually found my inner peace and a more normal physical condition.

I didn't do this by accident. Some issues needed to be resolved quickly. So, I decided to go at this speed, I asked to go at that speed and went for it. Sometimes our desire creates a lot better than we think.

In conclusion, taking your time to do this is a good thing. But this example is also there to give you one last important message; <u>the key is your desire,</u> your will, and just that. You just need to desire it to receive it. Your desire is creative.

YOUR DESIRE CREATES

I insist, do not make a belief of this. I do not want you to believe this statement. However, try to check if this is true in your life.

We believe so much in methods, that this idea may seem subversive, or even shocking. However, I noticed that the desire is the most important factor to create something. And I have only been able to realize this once I erased my beliefs. As before, for me, success was a matter of destiny, fate or belief.

You can verify this statement by studying the lives of those who do well in their lives. Did they apply a method? Did they struggle to reach their goals? Were they afraid of not succeeding? Did they have doubts, were they anxious and fearful? No doubt they did, but in the end they got there. So what was the main reason of their success, what preceded their efforts, their actions and even their beliefs? It is their desire, the desire to live this life, the desire to succeed, the desire to realize their dreams.

Desire is the foundation of everything you live. You just need to have a desire and to put it into practice.

But there is a pitfall. Our desires are themselves biased and influenced by our beliefs. Some of our desires are inadequate, toxic or unrealistic, others are too smothered by beliefs. To unlock the power of our desire, we must erase many beliefs.

Exercise

Erase all assumptions, prejudices, beliefs, certainties, knowledge, truths and convictions blocking your desire, preventing you from creating or manifesting itself in real life.

Erase all assumptions, prejudices, beliefs, certainties, knowledge, truths and convictions generating desires, which are toxic, dangerous or bad for others...

Erase all assumptions, prejudices, beliefs, certainties, knowledge, truths and convictions about desires, wanting, willing, longing for, and needing something.

Erase all assumptions, prejudices, beliefs, certainties, knowledge, truths and convictions preventing you from accepting your desires.

HOW TO WORK ON A SPECIFIC PROBLEM?

Now that you have discovered how to work on your beliefs in a comprehensive and systematic way, you can let the work within you carry on and see what changes for you. In general, this process takes several months, sometimes several years. It depends on where you started from, your enthusiasm, your ability to change, how open you are and on many other factors.

But now, you probably want to work on a specific problem in your life: love, work, money, security, family, health, friendships, hobbies, neighbors...

You can obviously extrapolate from all the examples I have previously given in this book, but some of you will probably be happy to start with a precise framework.

1. Start by identifying your problem

Be specific, write sentences on a sheet of paper, putting down everything related to it, what it implies, which are the reasons for you to have this problem and its consequences.

For example:
You have a problem with some neighbors; you cannot bear their behavior. They make too much noise, do not

134

lower the volume when you ask them to and they are unpleasant. It undermines you, it disturbs your sleep, it creates a considerable amount of negative emotions such as anger, rage, hatred, fear or sadness, it goes around and around in your head... Finally, you start feeling very uncomfortable at home and you want to leave. You have lost your inner peace and the trust you had in others, you do not feel respected and you find it unfair.

2. Say out loud what you want

Find what you really want concerning this problem. Do not try to go back to the old comfortable situation, but imagine the future you wish to have.

Very often, we think that all we want is for everything to be as it was before. But as you can see, life goes forward and not backwards, so it is better to find an objective that opens a door in the future.

For example:

I wish my neighbors could move away or I wish I could find a new apartment or I would like my landlord to find a solution and help me or...

3. Erase the beliefs that have created this situation

Generally, there are always initial, unconscious beliefs at the root of a problem, so it is very useful to erase the beliefs that have created the problem.

It is not always easy to find exactly what these beliefs are, but you do not need to find them. You just need to erase beliefs using the fact that your memory has associated them to your problem.

For example:
- *These things only happen to me.*
- *Life is unfair.*
- *Neighbors are always a problem.*
- *Landlords never care about their tenants.*
- *People have no respect.*
- *If there is a problem I am the person who will always suffer from it.*
- *I am never shown respect.*
- *I must be respected.*

4. Erase beliefs you have about this situation

It is very likely that the beliefs you have about your problem are preventing you from solving it. If you talk to someone about your problem you will always talk about your beliefs, thus it is a good time to be aware and then erase things.

Talking to someone and <u>listening to what you say</u> is a great way to find beliefs and solve your problems. Most of the time, when we talk we do not listen at all or we do not really listen however we draw our attention to what we will be saying later. Failing to find a solution is due to this lack of attention.

For example:
- *I'll never be able to resolve this problem, it is too complicated.*
- *I am sure that this problem cannot solve itself.*
- *People never make any effort.*
- *I can't count on my landlord, or on anyone else.*
- *The only solution would be to move (but by principle I*

refuse).
- It's my right to live here.
- I won't find any better anywhere else anyway.
- It's the same everywhere.
- People are idiots.

5. Erase beliefs preventing you from finding the solution

Often there are beliefs preventing us from finding the right solution. These beliefs may not be related to the situation, however they will still interfere with your thoughts and will block your intuition.

It is therefore useful to delete them.

For example:
- My life is made of perpetual problems, nothing will ever change.
- The problem is other people, not me.
- I am right and they are wrong.
- Inevitably, I am wrong and the others are right.
- I never win.
- Life is against me.
- God is against me.

6. Erase the beliefs preventing you from letting the situation resolve itself

Sometimes we obsess too much about doing, acting. We strongly believe that we must always do things and we assume that a situation cannot be solved without our intervention. However you probably know some people who let a rotten situation be and wait for it to resolve itself, don't you? And you may know people for whom it works. I know some people like that and for me it was a surprise to discover that behind their passive attitude there was a real philosophy: "it is not always necessary to act, sometimes it is better to let things be."

So I deleted my beliefs about the need to act and I felt more at peace. If we think that we must act or we believe that acting is always necessary, we move forward in an endless mental and emotional way, driving us to find a solution with our head whereas the solution to a particular problem cannot be found with our intellect.

Sometimes when the "fruit is ripe", the solution arises out of nowhere. Life can help you create, but it often moves slowly and sometimes others must see a lot of changes in their life before a solution emerges in yours.

For example:
Noisy neighbors could relocate for many reasons, some pleasant, some unpleasant. It depends on how good they are at creating their life, what they want and what they believe in. And all these things are not in your hands. But sometimes life subtly manages to intertwine stories bringing a happy ending for everyone involved.

We believe too much in: one man's meat is another man's poison. Although we can see this happening, we can also see – observing people's life without any belief – that what makes one person happy can also make someone else happy. There is not just one option available.

Creating a WIN-WIN situation, as they say in business, can generate positive changes for all parties involved. This can make us stop feeling guilty thinking that someone must be hurt so we can have what we want.

This way of thinking is one of the core beliefs we all have since birth: "we must suffer to evolve, we will inevitably miss something, life is hard, we must walk all over others to find happiness, we cannot compromise, we must sacrifice ourselves for others to be happy, nothing is ever easy... "

Exercise

Erase following assumptions, prejudices, beliefs, certainties, knowledge, truths and convictions:

- A problem never resolves itself.

- Action is necessary to solve our problems or other people's problems.

- Misfortune of one is the happiness of others.

- For me to win, someone must lose.

- You cannot have everything.

- There is no room for everyone on this Earth.

- To evolve or succeed we must suffer.

- Inevitably, I'll be in need.

- I must sacrifice myself for others to be happy.

7. The consequence is also the hidden cause of the problem

To my amazement, as I was progressing erasing beliefs, I started to understand that the moral or emotional consequence of a problem in life, was often what caused it.

Let me explain.

For example:

In the case of an issue with neighbors, here are some

consequences we could consider: we are pushed to our limits and we often feel powerless. We lose our inner peace; trust in people and in life. We are overwhelmed by a whirlwind of emotions and we often get mixed up, because we feel that our own security is threatened.

So we can look at the problem from this angle: there is a longstanding issue with security, peace and confidence in life within us. This issue may have been created during our childhood, before birth or we may have inherited it.

To understand this mechanism, just ask yourself what is the other event coming back to you when you think about this particular issue. Generally, we easily find some ideas. It can be a childhood event, an inability to defend ourselves against our brothers and sisters for example. Or it can be an event we cannot remember, which occurred before birth but which nonetheless exist e.g. your parents could tell you that they suffered from money problems during your mother's pregnancy. Generally, it is possible to connect several events to a problem we face in our current life. In this case, to heal, all these events must be corrected to restore a more stable and secure foundation within. Ideally it would also be a good idea to consult a psychotherapist who can work on memories of past events. But you can also delete beliefs associated with those moments at the source of this issue.

In the following parts of my method, I will give you the keys so you can do this yourself. However, nothing is better than talking to someone, someone who listens and who asks the right questions. Often, talking is enough to heal. You will be able to see this if you delete your belief about: "talking is useless"...

8. We must talk about our problem and express our emotions

Trying to give you explanations as thorough as possible, I am going slightly outside of the main subject of this book to introduce some elements that I will develop in my next books but nevertheless it is useful and necessary for you to understand the power of talking and expressing emotions.

Talking is a way to "let a certain pressure out". Each emotion generates an internal pressure. This pressure is able to change the way you think, feel and act. Your emotions have this power but they are that powerful only when they are not expressed.

Your emotions dissipate from the moment you express them. In ex-press, there is the prefix ex-meaning going outside, and -press, which is like pressing, pressure. When you express yourself, something is pushed out.

Emotions can be seen as a gas that occupies the whole of your body. When you express this gas, you let it go outside and from being harmful, it becomes harmless.

Sometimes, expressing emotions is a difficult exercise, it is a challenge.

For example: Are you able to say out loud to your parents that you love them?

This is a positive emotion, but how easy is it to do? Most people I asked this question to, have answered that it is actually something they never or seldom do. It's easier to do it in writing or it is something we only say when a difficult situation warrants it.

Why this embarrassment? Why this difficulty? Probably

because we have been educated to avoid expressing emotions. Children have the right to do it but when we grow up, this right is taken away from us. But why? It is due to beliefs from the society we live in. This can vary a lot from one country to another depending on cultural differences. I think you understand what I am trying to say.

Talking about your problems to friends, family, strangers, therapists or your doctor can help you feel better. Hence, you will find making good decisions and waiting easier to do.

But talking to someone about a very personal problem can be intimidating. In this case, talk to yourself, talk to God or to an imaginary friend. Talking to oneself may seem strange but the aim is to let go of the emotions that make your life a misery. Doing this is better than getting mixed up. When you do it, choose a quiet place where nobody can see or hear you and go for it! Be true, be honest with yourself, do not limit yourself to a certain wording, state all things coming to mind, it feels good!

We are particularly stuck on an emotional level. Freeing ourselves at this level is worthwhile. Do not try to be perfect with others and keep quiet. Do not try to solve your problem alone. Who says you have to handle it on your own, except you? Seek help and find help. And if it is difficult to find someone who can listen, delete the beliefs which may block you from finding that person.

9. There is no magic recipe

We also believe that there are miraculous cures to live our lives. We believe too much in methods. My method is just a tool to help you get better. There are other methods, but in the end, what matters most is you. It all depends on your intelligence, your intuition, your creation of life, your support network, how strongly you accept to change but also how you let life help you ...

OPENING YOURSELF

I have been erasing my beliefs for more than 20 years. And occasionally, I still delete something. I hope to have finished the day I die ;-)

Doing this has gradually changed how I see the world. I became more lucid, more pragmatic, I left behind all kinds of beliefs: superstitions, inherited beliefs, beliefs coming from science and also New Age ones I gathered through courses I followed or books I read. Relieved by all this, I discovered some amazing and certainly "incredible" things that allowed me to create this new way of healing, transforming and awakening, which I call «Doors of Consciousness».

I went through many changes in my body, my energy levels as well as my social and private life. I could tell you how I perceive time as an example. My perception has changed dramatically since I erased my beliefs about time. When everyone has the impression that time flies, I have rather the impression that every year lasts 10 years. Recently I had the impression that the last 6 years have lasted a whole life. This experience is neither good nor bad in itself, but it is a very strange feeling.

Working as a holistic practitioner, I have made extraordinary progress. I have discovered one thing after the other, and my view of the world, human beings, body and soul has changed. All these insights have helped me find new elements to erase, new ways to help people and improve efficiency. This work has been very demanding even exhausting at times, because I had been practicing every day for 10 years, 2 hours a day on average. A crazy task, 7'300 hours of personal work not including the time I devoted to my patients or courses I delivered.

I came to realize that to innovate, we must use our intuition and Consciousness **AND** have no beliefs. Beliefs are an enormous handicap when we want to find a new idea.

Whatever your profession, I think that erasing your beliefs will bring your talent, your knowledge and your skills to another level. You will be able to cross the barriers that we all put around us and be really original.

Some occupations are more likely to attract the "inventors" or "researchers". And others need people who know how to excel and to transcend themselves. If you work in that type of professional environment, erasing beliefs should significantly help you stand out.

Surely, erasing will not only help you at work, it will also be a precious help in your daily life, in your love life, in your family life and also with sports and hobbies.

I have noticed that, in order to make significant progress, it is best to erase beliefs as part of a daily routine. Beliefs can be found in your thoughts or your words at anytime. The best is to erase the belief as and when you are saying it or thinking about it. Otherwise you will quickly forget what you thought about or what you said, therefore if you leave these beliefs be, they will go back to your unconscious mind and will continue to influence you. Working on your beliefs on a daily basis, you will slowly start to change how you view the world and you will begin to transform your life.

But don't be afraid, you will still have an opinion on things! Getting rid of our beliefs doesn't mean that you cannot have an opinion or a point of view. Your opinion will simply be less rigid. You will be able to change it more easily, to question it and not get angry if someone contradicts you.

I will finish this book making an incursion in the imagination, forgetting for a moment that some things are impossible...

Imagine It Is always possible to choose the right till at the supermarket.

Imagine it is possible to eat anything but broccoli.

Imagine a world where there would be no problem to solve.

Imagine we stop believing that to win, someone else has to lose.

Imagine it's easy to find love.

Imagine something really going faster than light (even if we believe it is impossible, e.g. the quantum intricacy).

Imagine a stock exchange no longer governed by beliefs, emotions and greed.

Imagine politicians who no longer belong to a party, who would no longer debate endlessly about their beliefs but who would be really looking for the perfect solution using their intelligence and intuition at their best.

Imagine companies not seeking profit, but mainly trying to improve life on Earth by creating innovative, ethical, environmentally friendly, beautiful and well designed products.

Imagine planet Earth without beliefs.

Printed in Great Britain
by Amazon